Succe:

MW00986629

Grantwriting Beyond the Basics

BOOK 3:

Successful Program Evaluation

by Michael K. Wells, CFRE

Portland State University
Extended Studies
Continuing Education Press
Portland, Oregon

Michael K. Wells is a partner in Grants Northwest and has been consulting since 1987. He has worked with dozens of nonprofit organizations, health clinics, Native American tribes, and local governments and has helped them to raise over $50 million. He is a Certified Fund Raising Executive (CFRE) and teaches grantwriting at Portland State University. Michael is editor of the CharityChannel online *Grants and Foundation Review* and a board member of the Grant Professional Certification Institute.

Grantwriting Beyond the Basics, Book 3,
Successful Program Evaluation, 2007

ISBN 978-0-87678-120-3 (softcover)

Printed and bound in the United States of America
13 12 11 10 09 08 07   1 2 3 4 5 6 7 8

Continuing Education Press, Portland State University

Library of Congress Cataloging-in-Publication Data

Wells, Michael K., 1943-
    Grantwriting beyond the basics / by Michael K. Wells.—1st ed.
        p. cm.
    Includes index.
    ISBN 978-0-87678-120-3 (alk. paper)
    1. Fund raising.   2. Proposal writing for grants.   3. Nonprofit organizations—Finance.   I. Title.
    HG177.W45 2005
    658.15′224—dc22

                                                                    2004029303

Copies available from:
Portland State University
School of Extended Studies
Continuing Education Press
PO Box 1394
Portland, OR 97207-1394
P: 866-647-7377
F: 503-725-4715
www.cep.pdx.edu

Every effort has been made to provide current website information. All website URLs were current and correct at the time of publication. Due to the nature of the World Wide Web, URLs may change at any time and some pages may no longer be available. If a link does not work, try removing everything after the main address or do a web search for the agency name. Websites change more often than agencies.

We welcome any comments, suggestions, or ideas about this book. Please send them to press@pdx,edu, or mail them to PSU Extended Studies, Continuing Education Press, PO Box 1394, Portland, Oregon, 97207-1394.

Printed on acid-free paper.

Contents

SECTION TWO: Evaluation in Grant Proposals

Illustrations

Foreword

When I started writing grants 30 years ago, funders didn't routinely ask for proof that we were making a difference. Grantseekers were able to say, "Give us the money and we'll do this cool thing," and that was that.

Those days are gone.

Today, there is tremendous pressure, not only to articulate clearly the problem we're addressing and to quantify what we're going to do about it, but then to measure whether we affected any change. The pressure is coming from sources both inside and outside our organizations.

Michael's insightful book will help ease that pressure.

As you have probably experienced, grantwriters are often drivers of change in organizations, and nowhere is that more obvious than in program evaluation. If grantors didn't ask us to justify their support, many of our organizations wouldn't hold themselves accountable. So grantwriters, those of us with the most visceral relationship with grantors, are the ones asking the hard questions inside our organizations and, indeed, changing behavior.

At least as problematic as the requests from funders is the resistance we often encounter from our own staff, who often view evaluation as a test that they might not pass. They'll suggest the clients are too vulnerable to be asked how they're faring, or they'll say it's impossible to prove whether prevention worked, or they'll object that no one can quantify the impact of art. Often, those who raise money are considered "the dark side" of the organization, and we're told that client information is too confidential to be shared with us.

This book offers responses for each protest, and helps us show our colleagues why evaluation is in our own best interest, strengthening our programs, our organizations, and the outcomes of those we serve.

Once we start to evaluate our work, we discover it's hard to know just how to characterize effectiveness. For example, a woman had been working with a group of Native American fathers on early childhood parenting. On the last night of class she told them she was worried about how to measure the effectiveness of the program for the funder. From the back row came the quiet voice of a shy young man: "With all due respect, ma'am, you could ask us."

On the other hand, sometimes the outcomes are complex. An evaluator once asked a troubled and divided family how their counseling process had gone. "We hate that therapist," came their unified response. "She's no good, and we all agree that being with her was a waste of time!" So when the evaluator approached the therapist for her point of view, he was surprised to hear her say, "This process was a complete success!" A probing question revealed her rationale. "My goal with this family was to get a disparate, disconnected group of individuals to come together to fight a common enemy."

It's easy to get intimidated or overwhelmed when the situation requires scientific or statistical evaluation. We are, after all, usually writers and not scientists or statisticians. Our fears are quelled, however, by Michael's patient passages that make a daunting topic manageable. All three of Michael's books in the *Grantwriting Beyond the Basics* series have done the same thing—taken a subject a bit beyond our reach and brought it within our grasp, making us more competent and confident, and more able representatives of the important work of our sector. The best part is that he guides us through the hard parts with the familiar kindness of a wise old friend.

He brings just the right combination of experience and skill to the task. He's worked in nonprofits as staff, board, volunteer, and consultant, so he knows firsthand the quirks, fears and reservations people have about being judged. Stints in the business world have given him a results-oriented perspective. Over 20 years writing grants have taken him through the journey of learning his subjects from the inside out. The *Grantwriting Beyond the Basics* series takes this accumulated knowledge and lays it out for the reader.

As grantmakers grow more sophisticated and demanding about evaluation, it is incumbent upon us to help our organizations respond with skill and grace. The journey to effective evaluation may be arduous, but now we have a roadmap.

—*Susan Howlett*

Susan Howlett is a Seattle-based grantwriter, consultant, and trainer.
She is co-author of *Getting Funded: The Complete Guide to Writing Grant Proposals*.
Susan may be contacted at www.susanhowlett.com.

Introduction

For many grantwriters, evaluation competes with finances as the least favorite part of developing proposals. It seems terribly complex, it can feel like it's forced on you by funders, and you may experience resistance from the program people whose cooperation you need to develop a good proposal. The evaluation section is treated as a necessary evil and an afterthought—something you throw together after the real work of your proposal is done—so it is often one of the weakest parts of many grants. In a competitive funding round, a strong evaluation section may make the difference between getting funded or turned down.

Yet if you embrace evaluation and incorporate it into your grant development process, it will strengthen your whole proposal. You'll develop more compelling needs statements, create stronger goals and objectives, and write better narratives. Your proposals will be more fundable, and once funded, the grant programs will be more successful.

In fact, your whole organization will benefit, because evaluation is becoming more important not just in grant proposals but in all aspects of operation. The organizations that survive and thrive will be the ones that understand, measure, and work to improve themselves and their programs. And the way that's done is through program evaluation.

Successful Program Evaluation is intended to demystify evaluation and give you the tools to develop stronger grant evaluation sections. It will not tell you how to do a full-scale evaluation with statistical outcomes, which I believe requires more training than one book can promise (most professional evaluators are PhDs). As with financial statements, you don't need to be able to produce full-scale evaluations, you only have to understand evaluation enough to decide whether and how to approach it, and to be able to describe it.

Evaluation as a field is in flux and can be frustrating. There are different definitions for the same words and different words for the same thing. I found hundreds of Websites and downloadable articles; you could spend months just following links. I've tried to keep this book manageable and consistent, giving enough information but not too much.

As I got into this book, I realized how the depth and complexity of evaluation as an intellectual exercise could come to drive a grant project. Here are two principles that can help make your evaluation one of the most valuable parts of your work:

Use activity-driven evaluation, not evaluation-driven activities. Although it's important to be able to measure our work, the work itself is what's important, rather than the measurement. As we see in chapter 7, an evaluation perspective can greatly improve program activities, but resist the temptation to choose activities just because they're easy to measure. Instead, identify the most productive, meaningful activities and figure out how to evaluate them. As we'll see when we look at qualitative evaluation, it's possible to study something and see that it's worthwhile even if we can't get the results into numbers.

Measure what matters. Just as any major grant should grow out of your organization's mission, so your evaluation should measure progress toward achieving the mission. In a wonderful article called "Measuring what matters in nonprofits,"[1] the authors use the example of the Nature Conservancy. Its mission was "to preserve the diversity of plants and animals by protecting the habitats of rare species around the world," but it measured the numbers of acres it had acquired and was protecting. In the mid-1990s, the board realized that, while they were saving habitat, this wasn't necessarily preserving species diversity and, further, that they couldn't realistically evaluate how their work impacted all the biodiversity around the world. So they decided to measure how they were preserving biodiversity in the areas they did manage and changed their strategy from only acquiring land to protecting species, as well.

Your grant probably isn't going to cause a mission overhaul, but you can focus your evaluation on things that further your mission, rather than just what satisfies a funder.

In the words of Albert Einstein, "Everything that can be counted does not necessarily count; and everything that counts cannot necessarily be counted."

—*Michael Wells*
Portland, Oregon

---

[1] "Measuring what matters in nonprofits" by John Sawhill & David Williamson, *McKinsey Quarterly* 2 (2001). http://www.mckinseyquarterly.com

Acknowledgements

Dedicated to my daughters Maya, Melissa, and Julie. You've made me so proud and my life so rich.

Acknowledgements:

- Grantmakers for Effective Organizations (GEO) for use of their Due Diligence Tool

- The Evaluation Forum at Organizational Research Services, Inc., for use of their logic model examples.

Also, thanks to:

- Alba Scholz, publishing manager at Portland State University Continuing Education Press for making all this happen again

- Hilary Russell (content editor) and Cher Paul (copyeditor, indexer) for giving this book form, making it readable, and forcing me to use correct grammar

- Denise Brem (layout) and Michael Marshall (cover design) for making the book attractive and reader friendly.

Understanding Evaluation

Before You Start | 1

GRANTWRITERS AND NONPROFIT STAFF are increasingly called on to develop, or participate in, evaluations or studies. Most of us aren't trained researchers and approach the subject with some skepticism. We know it's going to take time and energy, and it's not clear what it gets us. This chapter gives some perspective before we get into the details of formal evaluation.

Why Do Evaluation?

The primary reason for *including evaluation in grant proposals* is that funders require it. Proposals with good evaluation sections score better and are more fundable than ones with poor (or no) evaluation sections. Being able to cite a positive prior evaluation of your existing program increases your chances of receiving future or continuation funding.

The primary reason for *doing evaluation of your program* is that it gives you reliable information to improve your program and services to your clients. Evaluation can provide data on whether a program works and why, which parts of it are effective and which need improvement, and whether it is the best use of your organization's scarce resources.

Notice that these are not the same. Fortunately, the "stick" of funder requirements and the "carrot" of program improvement both lead to the same place. Your job as a grant professional is to take advantage of the requirement and use it to improve your grant proposals and therefore your programs and possibly your organization, itself.

Beyond these two fundamental reasons for doing program evaluation, there are several more advantages to your organization both during grant development and during program implementation.

In grant proposals:

- Evaluation provides a framework for improving both your grant proposal and the project you're seeking to fund by providing measures to make your goals and objectives more meaningful.

- Evaluation provides a way to involve key stakeholders and direct service staff in program planning, which increases their buy-in into your program. A positive evaluation can help your organization attract new staff, volunteers, funders, and collaborators.

- Doing your own evaluation reduces the chances of funders or other outsiders undertaking their evaluation of your program, which might be less informed and more detrimental to your organization.

- A strong scientifically based evaluation can turn your innovative project into a research study, and could lead to it being named an "evidence-based practice."

In program operations (after you get funded):

- Evaluation gives immediate feedback, allowing you to identify and fix problems in existing programs while you still have grant funding to implement the changes.

- Evaluation provides a mechanism for getting feedback from your clients and/or participants about their perceptions of your organization and project, and a way of letting them know how the project is working. An evaluation showing that your program works can motivate your existing clients and attract new ones.

- Evaluation provides valuable information for longer-term strategic planning and program improvements.

- Evaluation provides solid data for disseminating information about your program, and for others who may want to replicate it elsewhere.

Resistance to Evaluation

Despite these advantages many nonprofit organizations and their staffs are resistant to, or suspicious of, evaluation for a variety of reasons. The grantwriter must often respond to these concerns, and even advocate for evaluation, in order to be able to develop a successful proposal. Here are six *common objections* to evaluation and *responses* you can use to overcome them. If these are your own beliefs, you'll need to think them through before trying to convince others.

Objection 1: Evaluation is a way to judge us, to label our program a success or failure, and perhaps punish us (i.e., cut our funding).

Assumptions:

- Evaluators are looking for a perfect program, and if we don't have it, we'll get marked down.

- Many people's only experience with evaluation has been employment performance reviews and college board tests. They are reluctant to be judged and ranked.

- If we can keep our program results fuzzy, "they" won't notice and we can keep doing what we're doing.

Responses:

- By looking at what works and doesn't work in a program, evaluation can be used to improve your services, not to punish your organization. Evaluation also helps you learn for whom, where, and under what circumstances did it work.

- Funders, management, and governing boards are looking for results. The lack of good program evaluation is worse than finding things that need improvement.

Objection 2: Evaluation is forced on us by the funders for their own purposes (like punishing us; see objection 1.)

Assumptions:

- Evaluation is something we wouldn't want to do if funders didn't make us. It has no intrinsic value to our organization.

Responses:

- If you design your own evaluation, you can have control over it, rather than ceding the control to others (like funders).

- If you do a good evaluation, it will help your organization improve its program, improve services to your clients, meet the funder's needs, and help you attract future funding.

Objection 3: Money spent on evaluation is diverted from direct client services, where it could be helping people.

Assumptions:

- Evaluation is expensive.

- Evaluation is always competing with services for the same funds.

- Evaluation doesn't help our clients.

Responses:

- Evaluation doesn't have to be expensive and sometimes has separate funding.

- A positive evaluation can help you raise more funds in the future.

- Evaluation can improve services and outcomes for your clients, making direct service dollars more effective.

Objection 4: We're "people people," not "science people," and we don't understand or like statistics.

Assumptions:

- Evaluation is all abstract, dry statistical stuff, not relevant to the actual work we do.

- The outside evaluator will look down on us or manipulate the data to make us look bad.

- This is complicated and we can't learn it.

Responses:

- At one time, evaluation was heavily statistical, but program evaluation is increasingly moving to qualitative measurement that looks at people's actual experience and the impacts of programs on their lives.

- Getting clarity about the uses of data and intentions for using findings in advance can help both the evaluator and program staff do a better job.

- A good evaluation process is designed to include program staff, and a good evaluation report is written for lay people to understand.

Objection 5: Evaluation will take staff time away from providing direct services.

Assumptions:

- The program staff only want to do their regular jobs and aren't interested in improving their services.
- The best use of staff time is working directly with clients, even if the work is less effective than it could be.

Responses:

- Evaluation data collection will take some of your program staff time—how much depends on the evaluation design.
- Staff time spent on a good evaluation will improve their work lives and the lives of their clients.

Objection 6: This is different than the way we've always done things, and we don't understand it or like it.

Assumptions:

- If we change, it may be uncomfortable.
- The way we do things is the best it can be; it doesn't need improvement.

Responses:

- This feeling may be the underlying basis for some of the first five objections.
- Doing evaluation may lead to change and may be uncomfortable, but it's worth it if the resulting improvements are real.
- With new information, nonprofits are discovering better ways of operating.

Do You Need a Formal Evaluation?

Before we look at evaluation in depth, let's step back a minute and think about how formal an evaluation you might want for different kinds of grant proposals or programs. Grants run the gamut from $1,000 projects to multimillion-dollar, multiyear complex social service programs. Obviously these can have very different evaluation needs, and small grants rarely require formal evaluation.

Many smaller funders, especially family foundations, want to see 100 percent of their money go directly to the people being served, and don't want anything spent on evaluation (although they would like to see some results). For these funders (and some other kinds of grants), the kind of structured evaluation process described in this book is overkill.

Let's be clear: You always want to tell funders what you're doing and how their support is helping your program. As with the thank-you letter you send upon receiving a grant, it builds their confidence in you and helps develop a relationship. But it doesn't have to be complex. For a small organization, a simple evaluation is better than no evaluation at all.

Performance Monitoring

In many cases, what you're doing is called *performance monitoring*, which answers the question, "Did you do what you said you would do?" This may involve collecting numbers, but it can also be a simple report that the project was completed and the money was spent correctly. Performance monitoring doesn't necessarily gather new data beyond what you're already collecting and rarely requires any analysis. Some types of grants where you would report performance include:

- **Small grants for program support:** These are often contributions based on belief in the organization rather than for a particular project.

- **Performing arts groups season support:** Another name for program support, you would report on audience size and critic's reviews.

- **Capital campaigns:** Generally capital grants are part of larger building campaigns, and the goals have been established in a case statement. Evaluation is often limited to whether construction is on time and on budget. There may be separate goals for building usage, but they will generally also be performance reporting, rather than analysis.

- **Equipment purchases:** These are similar to capital campaigns but on a smaller scale, such as the van example below.

Information you're already gathering for management purposes can be used for performance reporting of program support. For example:

- **Small theater group:** Numbers of tickets sold, size of audiences for particular shows, net income.

- **Skid row mission:** Numbers of meals served, clothes and blankets distributed, showers taken, bed nights.

- **After-school program:** Number of kids participating, kinds of activities, volunteer hours, trips taken, books read.

Piggyback Evaluation Reports

In some cases, you may be receiving both large and small grants for the same or similar programs. If you are already doing a large-scale evaluation for a major grant, take some of the evaluation results and insert them into a letter report to your small funders who are providing operating support.

Program Staff Evaluation Reports

Here's an example of a simple report that can be done by program or development staff: You apply for funding to buy a van to take kids on outings. The evaluation questions are, "Did you buy the van?" and "Are you using it to take kids on outings?" You could provide the funder with a list of outings, numbers of kids participating, and copies of the bill of sale and the vehicle title. You could spice it up with a picture of the van with happy children at the local science museum, maybe with the funder's name printed discretely on the van under your logo. This evaluation doesn't create any extra work, since it fits within existing program activities.

Board of Directors Evaluation Reports

For straightforward projects that have significant impact for the organization, I like to use the board of directors for evaluation. Your board's job is to oversee the work of your organization, so the regular program reports at board meetings should allow them to evaluate the project and implement improvements. Having the evaluation done by the board rather than staff adds some credibility. It also ties the grant project to other organizational work of the board such as policy and program decisions.

Often I will break board evaluation into two steps:

1. Did we do what we said we would do? Were the objectives accomplished—on time and within budget?

2. Did the project accomplish its purpose? Did we reach the goal, fulfill the need?

For example, consider a marketing and audience development program for a small orchestra. If you're mailing out brochures and your audience is growing, the board can track, measure, and evaluate these results. This type of evaluation is good for local foundations that like to fund direct program activities and may already be familiar with your organization.

Reporting on Internal Evaluation

Your organization may already be doing evaluation under another name. If so, you can use it as a built-in data collection system or even make it your entire evaluation. Two common internal systems are *quality assurance* (QA) and *continuous quality improvement* (CQI).

Quality Assurance

In health care, mental health, substance abuse treatment, and related fields, QA staff or committees are often required for licensure or accreditation. The committees generally include senior management, clinical directors, and program staff. They review things like data reports, client charts, staff performance, and client satisfaction. QA may be required in a grant as part of contract compliance. If your agency has a QA program, the information it is already gathering will be invaluable for developing your program evaluation—in fact, it may be all you need.

Continuous Quality Improvement

Developed by Japanese industry, CQI was based on the work of W. Edward Deming in the 1940s. Instead of collecting information centrally and periodically implementing major program changes, CQI involves the line staff and managers in constantly identifying problems and opportunities, and empowers them to implement changes without having to go to top management. Many nonprofits have started using CQI, and if your organization has a CQI program, it can be the basis of a formative evaluation. Sometimes QA programs incorporate CQI.

Organizational Commitment

A national organization I've worked with, the National Indian Child Welfare Association (NICWA), evaluates all aspects of its programs, including services, products, and events. This helps them guarantee quality services in support of their mission and assures their diverse constituencies and funders that their programs are effective and produce results. This commitment has helped NICWA build and maintain a national reputation as a leader in its field. When writing a major grant proposal, they expand their evaluation process to meet the needs of the program.

About Program Evaluation | 2

Basics of Evaluation

Nonprofits, foundations, and government agencies are increasingly focusing on program outcomes, cost efficiency, and organizational improvement. This is driven by increasing competition for decreasing funds, the application of business models to nonprofits, the general move toward accountability, and society's desire to see that the people served by social programs visibly benefit. Evaluation is how service agencies get the information to know if they're succeeding.

Webster's Dictionary defines *evaluate* as "to determine the worth of; to find the amount or value of; to appraise." Perhaps because of this, many people think of evaluation as judging whether or not a program is worthwhile. However, in grants and nonprofit management, program evaluation is better understood the way the U.S. Office of Justice Programs describes it:

> Evaluation has several distinguishing characteristics relating to focus, methodology, and function. Evaluation (1) assesses the effectiveness of an ongoing program in achieving its objectives, (2) relies on the standards of project design to distinguish a program's effects from those of other forces, and (3) aims at program improvement through a modification of current operations.

The Kellogg Foundation has this to say about program evaluation:

- Evaluation can be defined as the consistent, ongoing collection and analysis of information in decision making.

- Effective evaluation is not an "event" that occurs at the end of a project, but is an ongoing process that helps decision makers better understand the project.

- "Good evaluation" is nothing more than "good thinking."

Most grants are for programs, so *program evaluation* is what we're talking about. However, many funders talk about grant funding for *projects*. In grants terminology:

- A **program** is an ongoing system of services, often with its own goals, procedures, and frequently its own budget.

- A **project** is a time-limited intervention with planned activities that are aimed at achieving defined program outputs or outcomes.

For example, an organization might have an after-school program for young children and a grant-funded project to provide reading readiness skills. Don't let the words trip you up; the term *program evaluation* is almost universally used, whether the grant is technically for a program or project.

Choosing the Appropriate Evaluation

In developing a grant proposal, you'll need to decide which type(s) of evaluation you want. Your choice will depend on the audience and the purpose for doing the evaluation. You have three major decisions to make: the *purpose* of your evaluation, the *methods* you will use to gather and interpret data, and—for quantitative methods—the *design* of your component groups.

Purpose

The two main types of evaluation used for grants are *formative* and *summative*. They differ in their purpose and in when they occur. Formative evaluation helps you improve your program, and summative evaluation helps you prove whether the program worked the way it was planned.

- **Formative evaluation** begins early in a project and is used to make decisions about changes or improvements during program implementation. Its purpose is often internal to the organization, but it can also serve a funder who is looking for direct benefits to program clients. Formative evaluations usually provide monthly or quarterly reports about meeting program objectives, completing project activities, measuring participants' progress, and assessing staff performance.

- **Summative evaluation** may gather information throughout a project, but the results are used at the end to judge the success and impact of the project, based on its goals and objectives. Summative evaluation reports are based on formative information (e.g., quarterly reports) and follow-up data.

Depending on the type of evaluation you use, the sort of information needed will be different and so will the focus of your interview questions. Figure 2-1 shows some of the differences between the two forms.

Figure 2-1. Characteristics of Formative and Summative Evaluation

Formative Evaluation	Summative Evaluation
• Provides information to improve your program. • Generates periodic reports so information can be shared quickly. • Focuses on program activities, outputs, and short-term outcomes.	• Provides information to demonstrate the results of your program. • Generally, creates a final report. • Focuses on long-term outcomes and program impact.
Questions focus on *objectives*: • What did the organization do to promote the program? • Did participants demonstrate interest in the program? • Are participants satisfied with the program? • How is the program changing participants' attitudes toward their community?	Questions focus on *goals*: • Did the program reach its goal for numbers of participants? • What changes occurred in participants' knowledge of their community? • Did participants exhibit an understanding of how changing behavior is relevant to their lives and to the community?

Methods

Quantitative, *qualitative*, and *mixed methods* are defined by how information is collected and interpreted.

Quantitative methods (abbreviated QUAN) are focused on things that can be counted, compared, measured, and statistically manipulated, such as data from questionnaires, tests, standardized instruments, or program records. This kind of evaluation grew out of hard science and strives for precision in numbers or attributes that can be ordered sequentially. It focuses on what happened, but can be weak in explaining why.

Qualitative methods (abbreviated QUAL) are designed to capture the experience of participants in their own words, rather than in categories defined by the evaluator. It uses methods such as participant observation, interviewing, and focus groups. The results often do not have a direct numerical interpretation. It can give information on why the results happened.

Mixed methods are collections of information and that are subject to both quantitative and qualitative analyses. They build on the strengths of both methods: the quantitative precision of measuring what happened and whether a program succeeded, and the qualitative description of why the program worked or not. Evaluators are increasingly using mixed methods.

Design for Quantitative Methods

If you're using quantitative methods, you'll have to decide how to configure your comparison group: *experimental design* or *quasi-experimental design*.

Experimental design requires that there be a treatment group that receives program services (intervention) and a randomly assigned control group, chosen from the same population, that does not receive program services. This is the technique used in medical and other scientific research, and many agencies consider it the gold standard of evaluation research. It is the basis for defining an evidence-based practice (discussed further in a later chapter).

Quasi-experimental design also involves comparisons and is often used in social service evaluation, but employs different methods.

- **A nonequivalent control group** may be chosen for comparison. It shares critical characteristics with the treatment group, but is not chosen by random assignment. Comparison groups could be students at a school with similar characteristics to the school receiving services.

- **Pre- and post-program testing** uses the treatment group as its own comparison group by testing them before and after the program and looking for changes.

- Similarly, **interrupted time series (ITS)** uses the treatment group as its own control by comparing outcomes before and after the program.

Figure 2-2 describes several types of quasi-experimental design and notes the resource requirements of each.

Roots of Program Evaluation

Program evaluation grew out of research, and most evaluators were originally trained in graduate school as researchers in various fields. Social science research has developed two distinct research traditions, *quantitative* and *qualitative*.

Quantitative research is based on the natural sciences and views the world as a set of objective phenomena that can be observed, measured, and analyzed in much the same way as physicists or medical researchers do their work. It looks for factual data that the researcher can view in an objective and detached way, define, and measure in the same way their hard science colleagues do. In social sciences, this is commonly used in economics and demographics.

Figure 2-2. Some Typical Quasi-Experimental Designs

Type of Design	Description	Resource Intensity
Customer satisfaction surveys, post-program	Participants' self-report of satisfaction with services they received (e.g., quality, access, friendliness, impact).	Low
Post-program measures	Use of evaluation tools to describe outcomes (e.g., behavior, attitudes, experience, or knowledge) *following* a program.	Low
Pre- and post-program tests or interrupted time series (ITS)	Describes participants' scores on expected outcome variables (e.g., behavior, attitudes, experience, or knowledge) *prior* to a program and *following* completion of the program.	Moderate
Pre- and post-program measures with a comparison group	Same as pre- and post-program tests and ITS, but with the addition of collecting similar scores for a *comparison group*.	High
Post-program measures and benchmarks	Same as post-program measures, only similar scores are also collected from partner organizations or other targets selected for *benchmark* comparisons.	High
Pre- and post-program measures and long-term post-program measures	Same as pre- and post-program measures, with additional scores obtained again at a later point in time (e.g., six months, one year, two years).	High

Qualitative research sees the world very differently. It believes that social behavior must be understood from the perspective of the individuals and groups being studied. Furthermore, the researcher is seen as bringing beliefs, background, and perspectives that will affect his or her observations, and therefore scientific detachment is neither possible nor appropriate. The researcher must find ways to understand the worlds of program participants and the meanings they give to their experience, since their beliefs affect what they do, and what they do affects the programs outcomes.

These traditions are compared in Figure 2-3.

Conducting Quantitative Evaluation

Quantitative evaluation is designed like experimental research and requires a comparison group to measure program effectiveness. It gathers information that can be interpreted numerically. Data analysis techniques to show cause-and-effect relationships include descriptive statistics (averages, means, percentiles, and frequency) or inferential statistics (sign tests, linear regression, and chi-square).This generally requires structured instruments such as questionnaires or surveys so that all participants' answers can be accurately compared and given numerical values.

Figure 2-3. Characteristics of Quantitative and Qualitative Evaluation

Quantitative	Qualitative
• Asks "How much?" and "How frequently?"	• Asks "How?" and "Why?"
• Starts with a hypothesis	• Grows from observation
• Objective	• Subjective
• Uses deductive reasoning	• Uses inductive reasoning
• Larger sample sizes provide statistical validity	• Smaller sample sizes can be used • Doesn't need statistical validity
• Uses control groups for comparison	• The study group is the sample
• Measurable outcomes	• Observable outcomes
• Numeric reporting	• Descriptive reporting
• Factual and uninvolved	• Human face and "data rich" in details

Quantitative evaluation helps answer questions that involve:

- Understanding the quantities or frequency of particular aspects of a program (e.g., number of dropouts)
- Determining cause and effect statistically
- Comparing different programs that have the same goals
- Establishing numerical baselines (pre- and post-program tests).

Instruments for Quantitative Evaluation

Instruments for quantitative evaluation include *questionnaires or surveys, logs, observation,* and *secondary data.*

Questionnaires or surveys often offer choices such as:

- Checklists—Select one, or choose all that apply.
- Quality or intensity scales—5-N point scale or Likert scale—to measure client satisfaction or agreement with statements.
- Frequency scales—Number of events or activities.
- Story identification—Offer fictional scenarios, and participant indicates which they relate to; works well with children.
- Ranking—Rank preferences (first choice = 1; second choice = 2; etc.).
- Demographics—Age group, gender, race, ethnic group, level of education, income, etc.

When designing questionnaires it is important that questions are worded unambiguously so that answers are exhaustive (covering all possibilities) and mutually exclusive (no overlaps between categories). It is difficult to design good surveys, but sometimes you can find surveys designed by experienced evaluators that have been tested.

Logs are kept by program staff or participants and are self-reports tracking activities, attitudes, and movement over a specified period of time. Information gathered must be structured into categories in order to be quantified.

Observation by trained observers is used to assess services or aspects of programs that can be seen and categorized. Simple examples could be observing and recording the conditions of facilities, street cleanliness, and whether public buses are on schedule. More experienced observers would be needed to observe quality of care provided by program staff or the interactions of staff and clients. Trained clinicians would probably be needed for accurately observing mental health client behavior.

Secondary data is existing organizational records that can be reviewed and analyzed. Narrative data such as agency records, policies and procedures, and program descriptions can be read for historical background and context, but can also provide quantitative information such as quantity of work done, numbers of clients completing the program, and so forth. Reports with numerical data such as budgetary history and service provision and utilization reports can provide current or historical information for qualitative analysis.

Once the quantitative information is gathered, it is coded for input into a computer, entered into a statistical program spreadsheet, and then run for statistical analysis. We'll look at statistics in a later chapter.

Conducting Qualitative Evaluation

Qualitative evaluation is, well, qualitatively different from quantitative evaluation. In quantitative evaluation, the questionnaire design requires high-level expertise, but the specialized knowledge of the person mailing surveys or tallying answers doesn't matter as long as they are reliable and accurate. In qualitative evaluation, the individual data collector is of key importance. The skill of the interviewer or focus group facilitator will greatly affect the quality of the data collected. So can their gender, race, appearance, and personal biases. Although the information being gathered is subject matter specific and questions may be structured, the participant responses are more free form and open to interpretation.

Qualitative evaluation helps answer questions that involve:

- Understanding participants' or others' feelings or opinions about a program

- Understanding how the patterns of relationships develop within a program

- Gathering multiple perspectives to understand the whole

- Identifying approximate indicators that program participants are making progress.

Instruments for Qualitative Evaluation

Instruments for qualitative evaluation include *structured interviews* and *focus groups*.

Structured interviews are designed so that each interviewee is asked exactly the same questions, so that the answers are comparable. The questions will generally take four forms:

- *Situational*—The interviewer describes a situation and asks the interviewee what he or she would do about it.

- *Observational*—The interviewer asks the interviewee to reflect on the actions of a system, a program, or a third party.

- *Conceptual*—The interviewer asks the interviewee directly about their beliefs, personal philosophy, and how they intend to behave.

- *Behavioral*—The interviewer asks the interviewee about their past experiences, behaviors, knowledge, skills, and abilities.

Focus groups are groups of seven to ten people assembled to discuss a particular topic, facilitated by a trained moderator. They're generally chosen to be somewhat homogeneous, so that they will talk freely. (For example, a group of doctors and patients could be dominated by the doctors; or employees might be reluctant to speak freely in front of their bosses.) The moderator is completely neutral and does not show his or her opinion, but keeps the discussion moving and makes sure everyone gets to speak.

Focus group discussions are more free-form than structured interviews. There are no standard questions, but there are specific topics and items to be covered. It's part of the moderator's job to see that all the items are covered in the allotted time.

With both interviews and focus groups, the discussion is generally recorded. For one-on-one interviews, audio recording is sufficient, but with a focus group, a videotape makes it easier to tell who's talking when the discussion is transcribed. Sometimes a recorder also takes notes.

Both interviews and focus groups are data rich in that they contain lots of information that must be transcribed, categorized, coded into meaningful units, and interpreted. The data can be arranged hierarchically or diagrammed, but doesn't lend itself to statistical analysis. Because the process is subjective, different coders can interpret the same data differently. Thus, one of the challenges is establishing agreed-upon norms to achieve inter-coder reliability, that is, consistency in how the different coders work.

Evaluation Instruments

Several types of instruments are used to collect data for program evaluation. Figure 2-4 lists some characteristics of the most common ones, including whether they apply to quantitative or qualitative methods or both.

Research Design Symbols

Researchers and evaluators sometimes use symbols to represent research design. Figure 2-5 shows some of the most common ones.

Evaluation of Economic Costs

Governmental and some private funders are increasingly looking for evaluation of the economic costs of producing program outcomes. The primary measures used are *cost-benefit analysis* and *cost-effectiveness analysis*.

Cost-benefit analysis estimates the costs and benefits of a program to society, translated into monetary terms. The calculation is Benefit ÷ Cost = Cost Benefit, with the assumption that if the ratio exceeds 1, the program is socially useful (high ratios are desirable). Cost-benefit analysis has some problems. It is of course difficult to convert some intangibles into monetary terms; outcomes are long-term, while costs may be short-term; it's difficult link long-term outcomes to the program. Cost-benefit analysis is typically prospective and used for planning major capital investments.

Cost-effectiveness analysis compares the financial costs of different programs with the same outcomes to one another. It doesn't judge the social value of the programs; it focuses on activities, outputs, and outcomes as units, and looks at which program produces more units for the same cost. Cost-effectiveness is typically retrospective and is used for evaluating discrete interventions.

Figure 2-4. Types of Evaluation Instruments

Instrument and Research Type	Characteristics	Advantages	Disadvantages
Surveys • Paper • Telephone • In person • Web-based *Quantitative*	• Self-administered (paper, Web) or staff-administered (telephone, in person) questionnaire • Multiple choice or short answer	• Ensure anonymity • Inexpensive • Easy to analyze • Can get lots of data • Can use existing questionnaires	• Need to get wording right • Impersonal • May need sampling expert for analysis
Interviews • In person • Telephone • Group *Quantitative or Qualitative*	• Generally hour-long meeting between evaluation staff and interviewee • More or less structured • Group interview is more structured than focus group	• Get wider range and depth of information • Builds client relationship • Can be flexible • Data rich	• Time-consuming • Skilled and appropriate interviewer is key • Hard to analyze and compare • Interviewer can bias answers
Focus Group *Qualitative*	• Informal, small group (7–10) of similar participants led by neutral facilitator • Discussion is led, but free-flowing	• Quick and reliable way to get participants' impressions • Rich and deep data source • Can convey key data not captured numerically	• Difficult to schedule • Group mix is important • Need skilled and experienced facilitator • Can be hard to analyze
Observation • Standard • Time-sampling *Quantitative or Qualitative*	• Systematic technique by trained observer, using standardized ratings to information	• View program in operation • Can adapt to events as they occur • Rich and abundant data	• Observations can be difficult to interpret and categorize • Multiple observers affect reliability • Can influence client behavior
Tests • Knowledge • Achievement *Quantitative*	• Pencil and paper or online achievement or aptitude tests	• Many standardized tests available	• High scores don't necessarily mean tested knowledge can be applied
Secondary (documentary) data *Quantitative*	• Review and analysis of existing agency records	• Comprehensive and historical information • Doesn't interrupt program • Information already exists • Can compare to or supplement primary data	• Time-consuming • Information may be incomplete • Inflexible (data already exists)
Journals *Qualitative*	• Personal, written observations by individual clients or staff, recorded regularly	• Give personal perspectives • Assess subtle changes in program over time	• Time-consuming • Some individuals unwilling to invest time • Difficult to interpret
Case studies or chart reviews *Quantitative*	• Individual client's case files • Information on such things as health conditions	• Can get specific data on results of treatment or program	• Need to protect confidentiality • Documents can be disorganized or unavailable
Critical incident report or Log *Qualitative*	• Document compiled by program staff during program implementation • Identify events that accelerated or slowed reaching goals	• People can describe unique situations in their own words	• Time-consuming • Some individuals unwilling to invest time

Figure 2-5. Common Symbols to Represent Research Design

Symbol, Examples of Use	Definition
X	Treatment or intervention: your program (sometimes a T)
O	Observation of measurement: O1 is first observation, O2 is second, etc.
Δ	No treatment or control group (sometimes left blank)
R	Random assignment from equivalent group (true experimental design)
C	Cutoff: Potential subjects are tested to see if they reach a cutoff point to be assigned to program or comparison group.
N	Nonequivalent group: Similar but not perfectly matched; e.g., matched for age and gender but not income.
O1 X O2	One group, pre- and post-program testing
X O X O	Static group comparison
O1 O2 O3 X O4 O5 O6	Interrupted time series (ITS)
R O1 X O2 R O1 Δ O2	Randomly assigned groups for pre- and post-program testing
N O1 X O2 N O1 Δ O2	Nonequivalent groups for pre- and post-program testing
C O1 X O2 C O1 Δ O2	Cutoff assigned groups for pre- and post-program testing

Cost-effectiveness analysis is more useful to evaluation, and often when a cost-benefit study is called for, a cost-effectiveness study is what is actually wanted. It is important to be clear about this if you are asked to evaluate the economic impact of a program. Cost-effectiveness analysis aligns with value-for-money auditing, as shown in Figure 2-6.

Figure 2-6. Cost Effectiveness and Value-for-Money Auditing

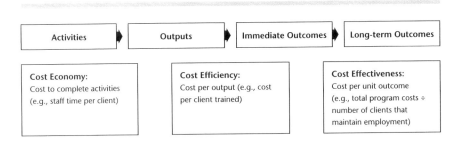

Evaluation Considerations | 3

BEFORE YOU BEGIN PLANNING your evaluation, there are a few concepts you need to consider: *evaluability*; *reliability and validity*; *confidentiality*, *anonymity*, and *privacy*; and in some cases *human subjects* and *cultural competence* issues. If you understand these and make the decisions about them beforehand, your evaluation will go more smoothly.

Evaluability

Can this program be meaningfully evaluated, and at what level? Any program can be evaluated, but if the results are not likely to be used in decision-making, or are too vague to be useful, the evaluation can be a waste of time. Program evaluability is determined by six primary criteria:

- Are program goals and objectives well defined and measurable?

- Are the program goals plausible and achievable, given the organization's capability and the funding available?

- Can the relevant performance data be obtained at a reasonable cost, within the grant budget?

- Do you have the resources, both financial and human, to carry out the type of evaluation being considered?

- Have the intended users of the evaluation results agreed on how they will use the information?

- Would any internal or external conditions, such as political or cultural factors, affect the ability to carry out a meaningful evaluation?

If you're able to answer these questions, it will be much easier for an evaluator and your organization to agree on the type of evaluation, its methods, and the intended uses of evaluation information.

Reliability and Validity

These concepts come from scientific research and are vital to effective evaluation. For an evaluation to show that a program caused the desired outcomes, its findings must be reliable and valid.

Reliability is whether the instrument gets the same results when repeated under similar circumstances over time. Threats to reliability include:

- Different interviewers working on an evaluation, who might interpret responses differently.

- Performing evaluation activities at different times. For example, a survey distributed in the morning or on a weekday might reach different groups than in the afternoon or on the weekend.

- Using different methods to collect evaluation data. If you use a fill-in-the-bubble survey one time and conduct interviews the next, the results may not be comparable.

Validity is whether the instrument actually measures the variables it was designed to measure. Threats to validity include confounding conditions and alternative explanations:

- If clients are receiving multiple services, it may be difficult to ascribe a particular outcome to any one of them.

- If the criteria for selecting clients for different programs are inconsistent, the results can't be shown to work with an identified group.

- Situation effects, such as subject comfort with the location of an interview, can affect their responses.

- If too many people drop out of a program (attrition rate), it can't be accurately measured.

- Client characteristics such as age, sex, race, or ethnicity can affect results. For example, if the respondents to a clinic's health survey have an average age of 22 one day and 64 the next day, the results will be different, and that difference can't be ascribed to the program being evaluated.

- Alternative explanations include external events or circumstances that could have caused the outcomes. For example, crime reduction could be attributed to community policing, but might also be affected by an aging population, gun control laws, economic conditions, or other factors.

To conclude that a program caused the desired outcomes, known as *causal inference,* five requirements must be satisfied:

- The expected relationship demonstrates a theoretical or practical basis.
- The program must precede the outcome in time.
- Alternate explanations for the outcomes must be ruled out.
- Program activities and outcomes must demonstrate a clear association.
- The outcome measures must be reliable and valid.

Findings can be reliable but not valid. If your scales consistently say you weigh 130 pounds, when actually you weigh 155 pounds, it is reliably giving the same results, but the results are invalid. However, for something to have validity, it must have reliability.

Confidentiality, Anonymity, and Privacy

If program clients or interview respondents are to provide honest feedback relating to the services they receive, they need to know that the information they share will not be associated with them outside of the evaluation team (and maybe not even within it). Confidentiality and anonymity are not the same thing:

Confidentiality means that the information can be traced back to the individual, but that their identity will not be known outside the evaluation team. Code numbers are commonly assigned to participants to secure confidentiality. In situations where people come in personal contact, such as interviews or focus groups, confidentiality is used.

Anonymity means that the information cannot in any way be traced back to the individual who provided it, whether inside or outside the evaluation team. Self-administered surveys with no identifying information is a common way to ensure anonymity.

HIPAA, the Health Insurance Portability and Accountability Act

A privacy provision of the Health Insurance Portability and Accountability Act of 1996, which requires healthcare providers to provide security for their patients' records, has had major implications for agencies providing any health-related services (including mental health or alcohol and drug treatment). Many federal grant RFPs include HIPAA requirements. Many major health care organizations have information about the implications of HIPAA on their Websites, including privacy and security information for clients and staff. One example, from the Oregon Health & Science University, is at www.ohsu.edu/cc/hipaa.

Human Subjects Issues

If you are applying for a federal grant or if you plan to report your evaluation findings outside your organization, you may have to submit your evaluation plans to an institutional review board for human subjects review and get your participants' informed consent to participate in your evaluation.

Institutional Review Boards

Institutional review boards (IRBs) are intended to ensure the protection of the rights and welfare of human subjects involved in research. Because some evaluation methods can be considered as research, it's valuable to put your evaluation plans through the review process so that you can disseminate your findings in the future, if you want to do so.

Most universities manage an institutional review board for their own research, and they are willing review the documentation of your evaluation strategy, data collection methods, and plan for analysis and reporting, usually for a fee. Many teaching hospitals and independent research organizations also have IRBs that nonprofit organizations may access. To find the IRB at a university, contact their Office of Sponsored Research.

An IRB human subjects protocol will generally fall under one of four categories:

- **No review:** If the data from your evaluation will not be published or otherwise distributed, no review is required. However, if you don't get a review and decide in the future that you want to distribute the results, you will need to defend the lack of review process.

- **Waived:** Many evaluation instruments such as surveys, interviews, and public observation qualify for a waiver of review under federal regulations and can undergo a certification by one member of the IRB, rather than a full review.

- **Expedited review:** Research or evaluation activities that carry minimal risk, and in which human subjects will be minimally involvement in standard methods, may receive expedited review by the IRB.

- **Full review:** All federally funded proposals, regardless of the type of study or whether the federal funding is direct or pass-through, must undergo a full review.

For more information on the protection of human subjects in research, go to www.hhs.gov/ohrp/humansubjects/guidance/45cfr46.htm.

Many universities offer training in IRBs and human subjects review. The University of Virginia has an excellent one, which includes an online

tutorial on human subjects reviews at www.virginia.edu/researchandpublic
service/irbsbs/index.html.

Informed Consent

To collect information from an individual, human subjects protection
requires that they give informed consent. Informed consent requires that the
individual is given complete information regarding the evaluation and his/her
participation in it. Consent must be obtained under circumstances that
provide the person sufficient opportunity to decide whether or not to
participate, as well as the guarantee that nonparticipation will not result in
denial of services or other negative consequences. Check with your funder
to see if they require that participant consent forms be kept on file.

When evaluators are employees of the organization being evaluated, and
the information comes from its records, obtaining information is not likely
to be a problem. With outside evaluators, agency employees may need to
transcribe pertinent information without providing individual identifiers.

Be aware of these special circumstances:

- Agreement to participate may imply consent as when people return
  a survey, agree to an interview, or accept an invitation to participate
  in a focus group.

- When working with children under age 18, parental consent is
  always required.

- A signed consent is required to use methods such as document
  review, observation, critical incident reports, or personal journals.

- For some research, obtaining authorization is impossible or simply
  not feasible. For instance, some epidemiological studies might access
  hundreds of thousands of records. In these cases, you may apply in
  writing for a waiver of authorization from the IRB.

Cultural Competence

Cultural competence is increasingly recognized as vital to conducting
accurate and valid program evaluation, especially qualitative evaluation.
This is important in both evaluation design and implementation, so that
participants feel comfortable and findings are accurate. Cultural awareness is
not limited to racial or ethnic groups, but also extends to sexual minorities,
immigrants, and people of different educational or income levels or classes.

When assessing the cultural competence of your proposed evaluation, consider these three areas:

- **Communication style:** This will affect the instruments you select. Some cultural groups prefer private conversations, others are more comfortable in small groups. Some groups prefer verbal to written communication. Some groups feel that direct eye contact is disrespectful, whereas others consider it a sign of honesty or sincerity. The evaluator should understand cultural norms.

- **The evaluator:** The person administering the instrument must be someone the participants will feel comfortable sharing personal information with, in terms of status, race, gender, or other character-istics. Sometimes an interviewer of the same sex or ethnic group will get very different answers than a person from another group.

- **Language:** If your program crosses cultures, be sure to invite the input of all groups by using evaluation instruments in the appropriate language(s). To the extent possible, consider not only the language but also the cultural norms of communication style.

Statistics and Data Analysis | 4

ONCE YOU'VE GATHERED your evaluation data, you'll want to figure out what it means. The process of determining meaning is data analysis, and it can be basic or highly statistical. In this book I'll look at some basic statistical analysis and describe some more advanced tools. For advanced statistics, you'll want to use a professional evaluator or researcher.

To do data analysis, an evaluator needs a data analysis plan. If you're using existing instruments, the developer may have provided a data analysis plan. If you have developed your own instrument, you'll have to develop your own analysis plan. The plan will depend on the type of questions you want to answer.

For example, for questionnaires with three choices (a, b, c):

- If you want to know the number of people who answered each question, you'll use a simple count.

- If you want to know how many people answered a, b, or c, you'll use a frequency distribution.

- If you want to report what percentage of people answered a, b, or c, you'll use a percentage distribution.

When testing participants' knowledge about a subject:

- If you want to know an average score, you'll figure a mean.

- If you want to know the change from a pre- to a post-program test, you'll figure a change in scores.

If you're doing qualitative evaluation with open-ended questions, you'll do a content analysis.

Levels of Measurement

The first concept for understanding statistics is levels of measurement, which refers to the mathematical precision with which the values of a variable can be expressed. There are four levels of measurement. Nominal variables are qualitative, the other three are quantitative.

Nominal variables are descriptive, and no numeric value or ranking is assigned to them. Examples are male and female or American and Canadian.

Ordinal variables are things that can be ranked or ordered, but do not have numeric precision. Examples are small, medium, and large.

Interval variables and **ratio variables** have meaningful and equal distances between values. An interval value has no true zero; a ratio variable does. Temperature is an interval value; zero degrees does not mean there is no temperature. Donuts are a ratio value; zero donuts means there are no donuts.

In most evaluations, interval and ratio values are treated as equivalent. However for mathematical purposes they are different: Both can be added and subtracted, but only ratio values can be meaningfully multiplied and divided (and therefore form ratios).

Finally, a ratio or interval variable can be reorganized into an ordinal or nominal variable. For example, participants' actual age distribution can be reorganized as older, middle-aged, and younger groups or as the 0–29, 30–59, and 60+ groups.

Descriptive Statistics

Descriptive statistics are used to describe the distribution of, and relationships among, variables. They are used when we are describing a population directly, and are usually concerned with only one variable. Many of them are simple calculations that a person without any statistical training can make.

Frequency Distribution

Frequency distribution is used to show how a population breaks down in whole numbers. As Figure 4-1 shows, there are four basic types:

- **Frequency distribution (FD):** The number of cases per category.

- **Cumulative frequency distribution (CFD):** The number of cases per category, adding each to the previous total.

- **Percentage distribution (%D):** The listing of proportions of each category.

- **Cumulative percentage distribution (C%D):** The proportion of cases per category, adding each to the previous total.

Figure 4-1. Examples of Frequency Distribution

Day	FD	CFD	%D	C%D
Monday	20	20	10%	10%
Tuesday	40	60	20%	30%
Wednesday	40	100	20%	50%
Thursday	50	150	25%	75%
Friday	50	200	25%	100%
Total	200	—	100%	—

Summary Statistics and Measures of Central Tendency

Summary statistics focus attention on particular aspects of a distribution and facilitate comparisons among distributions. For example, if you wanted to report the variation of income in the 30 counties in your state, you would be better off presenting average incomes; most people would find it difficult to follow a chart showing 30 frequency distributions, although they could easily comprehend a list of average incomes.

Summary statistics are generally presented as measures of central tendency, which are usually summarized with one of three statistics: the *mean*, the *mode*, or the *median*.

- **Mean**, or arithmetic average, is computed by adding the value of all cases and dividing by the total number of cases, e.g., (1 + 2 + 4 + 5 + 8 + 10 + 12) / 7 = 6. The mean is used for interval or ratio data and is the base for more complicated statistics such as standard deviation and t-tests.

- **Mode** is the most frequent value in a distribution. In this group (1, 2, 3, 2, 4, 2), 2 is the mode. It can be used for nominal data, such as the most common ethnic group in a given school, where ordinal or higher data wouldn't apply.

- **Median** is the position average, or the point that divides a distribution into two equal parts (also known as the 50th percentile). For example, in a group of seven (1, 2, 4, 5, 8, 10, 12), the median is 5. The median is used for ordinal or higher-level data. It is less affected by extreme values than the mean, so it is commonly used for measures such as household income.

The mean, mode, and median each have limitations and advantages, so in some cases you should consider reporting more than one measure of central tendency to provide a more accurate picture of the data.

Measures of Dispersion or Variability

The central tendency is only one aspect of a distribution and may be just one piece of the total picture. For example, let's consider three neighborhoods: one has 50 middle-class families; another 30 lower-class, 10 middle-class, and 10 upper-class; and a third has 35 lower-class and 15 upper-class. They might have about the same mean and median incomes, but widely varying social structures.

These differences can be captured with statistical measures of variation. Four popular measures of variation are the *range, interquartile range, variance,* and *standard deviation.*

- **Range** is the simplest measure of variation—for example, the age range among participants. It is calculated as the highest value minus the lowest value, plus 1.

- **Interquartile range** is the distance between the values of 75th percentile and the 25th percentile. It helps to eliminate the extreme cases on both ends (outliers) and focus on the core data; in our age range example, it removes the oldest and youngest participants. It is calculated as the 75th percentile minus the 25th percentile plus 1.[2]

- **Variance** takes into account the amount by which each case differs from the mean, and is mathematically the average squared deviation of each case from the mean. It is key to the development of other measures like standard deviation, although it is clumsy and time consuming to perform by hand. Most statistical computer programs have a function for figuring both variance and the related standard deviation.

- **Standard deviation** is the measure of the dispersion of scores around the mean or average. It is calculated as the square root of the variance. The standard deviation is used by statisticians to determine how confident they can be that some value of a random sample falls within a particular range; a smaller standard deviation gives a higher confidence in the accuracy of the statistic.

---

[2] Quartiles are the percentages that divide a distribution into quarters: 25, 50, and 75 percent of the cases.

Inferential Statistics

Inferential statistics are an attempt to make mathematic generalizations about a larger population from a smaller randomly collected sample. Its applications involve hypothesis testing and the examination of statistically significant differences. It involves the use of experimental designs and many specified procedures, often involving statistical software, and the statistics are beyond the scope of this book.

A basic question of evaluation is "How do things change together?" Association and correlation are two related but different ways of measuring this change. **Association** refers to the fact that two variables are related and change together. **Correlation** goes into more detail and tells the direction (positive or negative) and significance of the associations (statistically significant or not).

Hypothesis testing includes the development of a research hypothesis and null hypotheses about an association, which are to be tested and determined as "reject" or "fail to reject" at a certain level of confidence. When an evaluator feels reasonably confident (generally at least 95% confident) that an association was not due to chance, it is said that the association was statistically significant. There are several standard tests for statistical significance; they measure either significant association or significant difference. These tests, based on the kind of data available, are summarized in Figure 4-2 below.

Figure 4-2. Tests for Statistical Association

Level of Measurement	Test for Significant Association	Test for Significant Differences
Nominal	Mean, mode, median, range, percentage, chi-square	Chi-square
Ordinal	Spearman's rho, Kendall's tau	Mann-Whitney U test
Interval and Ratio	Pearson's r	t-tests, Z test, F test, ANOVA

Analyzing Qualitative Data | 5

QUALITATIVE EVALUATION deals with the actual experience of program participants. Qualitative data generally comes in narrative form collected from open-ended interviews, focus groups, journals, or logs. As stories or vignettes, this information can be used as anecdotes for giving a human face to an evaluation report or for showing examples of program success.

Qualitative data is not numeric, so it is not directly subject to statistical analysis. However, qualitative data that has been systematically collected can be processed and used to report outcome results. The process is laborious and time consuming because the first step is accurately transcribing the text from the interviews. The next step is coding or categorizing the information by common themes, which can be used to make general statements for each category. The results can be interpreted in various ways.

Thematic Content Analysis

Thematic content analysis involves reading and re-reading the data and identifying emergent themes and patterns, then using the themes for organizing the data. If you have different sources of data such as observations, interviews, and document review, it can provide rich, multilevel material that can increase the validity of your findings.

- **Determine the categories** for your analysis. **Predetermined categories** can be selected before the data is transcribed. They may be determined based on their importance to the program, or because they were included in the question that generated the responses. **Emergent categories** are determined after reading the transcribed data and are based on patterns in different respondents' answers.

- **Develop a category system.** Divide the data into meaningful segments, blocks of text that describe what is to be measured, including *who* said *what*. These units of analysis are the category descriptions that the evaluator who analyzed the text has created.

- **Place respondents by category.** Read the text of each of the respondents and place their responses in the appropriate category, coding them by key words, themes, numbers, or colors that relate to identified ideas.

- **Place responses by category.** Re-read the text and place the responses in the appropriate category, coding them by key words, themes, numbers, or colors that relate to identified ideas. Some codes will partially or completely overlap, with segments of text having more than one code attached to them.

- **Count the responses.** After all respondent responses have been reviewed and categorized, count the number of respondents and responses in each category.

- **Write a composite response.** Draft a general statement that reflects the content of all responses in each category. When responses are complex or include extensive data, a short paragraph may provide a clearer statement of the information provided.

Constant-Comparative Method

In this method, data and preliminary interpretations are constantly compared with each other. New data is compared with preliminary interpretation, then revised and repeated to create increasingly accurate descriptions and increasingly valid interpretations.

Grounded Theory

The goal of many qualitative researchers is to create grounded theory by inductively building a systematic theory that is grounded in, or based on, their observations and analysis. Observations are summarized into conceptual categories during program implementation, which are then tested directly with more observations. Over time, as the categories are refined and linked, a theory evolves. The evaluators refine their definitions of problems, concepts, and selected indicators. They then check the frequency and distribution of phenomena that would support or disprove the theory.

Grounded theory can be used to develop a program theory and logic model for a program. A logic model developed before the program begins can also be used to focus data collection and can be refined or revised to fit observed behaviors or outcomes.

Enumerating and Diagramming

Enumerating is a process for quantifying qualitative data. An evaluator might count the number of times a code is applied to data, the number of positive or negative comments, or other measures. It allows the data to be shown graphically.

Diagramming is the process of making a sketch, drawing, or outline to show how a program works or to clarify the relationship between the parts and the whole.

Evaluation in Grant Proposals

What Funders Want | 6

WHEN I WAS RESEARCHING the previous book in this series, *Understanding Nonprofit Finances*, developing the section on "What Funders Want" was fairly straightforward. Virtually all private foundations and corporate funders ask for audits or standard financial statements and project budgets in their application guidelines. Government funders are even more prescriptive, providing required budget categories and forms. When I interviewed foundation staff, they had a lot to say about what they look for in these financial documents.

Evaluation has proved to be a different story. The federal government makes very clear what they want, but among foundations, there aren't generally agreed upon requirements for evaluation sections in grant proposals. I knew from writing hundreds of grants that many foundations either don't specify evaluation in their guidelines or do so only in the most general terms.

Foundations

When I started talking to foundation staff, at first they professed little interest in evaluation sections in proposals. Certainly they aren't used to seeing the kind of formal evaluation sections described in this book. But when I asked further questions, it was clear that they want to know the results of the projects they fund, and they reward the applicants who plan to track and provide those results.

So how should you approach evaluation in a proposal to a foundation that doesn't provide clear guidelines? Here are notes from my discussions with program officers at a couple of local foundations, and their application guidelines. I've included their entire guidelines, not just the evaluation section, because you need to think about how the evaluation fits into the whole project when planning your strategy.

Martin Foundation

Interview: When I interviewed the program officer of this large general purpose foundation, I asked:

- If they used the GEO Due Diligence Tool (explained in detail later in this chapter). She responded, "Over the years, we have developed a very similar criteria for due diligence to those described in GEO's publication, and in fact, a nonprofit wanting to understand what we look for in proposals would be well served by reviewing the GEO Due Diligence Tool. Like GEO, we recognize that formal evaluation is often prohibitively expensive for grantees, but we put a lot of emphasis on strong program design and clearly defined outcomes."

- If they looked for cost effectiveness in proposals. She said, "Of course the foundation wants to be assured that its funds will be used efficiently, and we look for evidence of that. However, we also understand that some types of services may have a high cost per person served, but can nevertheless be delivered efficiently and effectively. In other words, we definitely look for a good return on the foundation's investment, but that can mean very different things depending upon the specific project."

- If they recommended logic models. She replied, "We don't require logic models, but we absolutely look for logical program design and a clear and cogent plan of action to achieve specific outcomes. Some organizations may find a logic model helpful to think through program design."

- What they look for in goals and objectives. She said, "We understand that it is often much easier to measure outputs than outcomes, especially for grant periods of three years or less. Nevertheless, we want to know specifically how an applicant intends to measure the success of the proposed project. Often we get proposals that spend more time describing the need for the project than describing the plan of action and how it will meet that need. That was one reason for adding the Project Effects tool to our online application. It is also important to point out that we understand that projects sometimes don't work out as planned. In those cases, we look for three things: prompt notification of the funder, learning from the attempt, and a course correction as a result of the lessons learned."

- If they look for best practices or evidence-based practices. "During the due diligence process, program officers research what are considered best practices in the field. At a minimum, we expect applicants to know what accepted best practices are for their field. If they are doing something different, they should be able to present a compelling rationale for their approach and, again, have a strong project plan and clear measures of success."

- If they fund evaluation. "Many of the foundation's grants support capital projects or capacity building where the outcomes are unequivocal—the building gets built, hopefully on schedule and on budget, and functions well for its purpose. Or the new staff is able to work with the board, constituency, and community to increase earned and/or contributed income that helps to sustain the organization's mission. Outside evaluation is helpful for projects that attempt major systems or social change. Often, the foundation is a co-investor with foundations that require and fund such evaluations. If an applicant made a strong case for funding for outside evaluation, it would be considered in the context of the full proposal."

In conclusion, the officer said, "Remember that your organization's relationship with the Martin Foundation is going to extend over a long period of time and that you may want to apply again in the future. Each application and funded project helps form an impression of your organization. The credibility of your organization will be strengthened by meeting its goals and objectives."

Martin Foundation's Online Application Form: This form has places for the project's effects on the organization's size, full-time equivalents (FTE), and structure; its programs, operating expenses, and ability to generate income; and the issue or need the project addresses. There is a text box for each topic.

Needs Statement

Explain the need for the project, and why it is important. If appropriate, comment on past or present attempts by the applicant and others to address this need.

Project Description

Describe the project, including its goals and specific objectives. Explain how the project will be implemented over time. Explain why your organization decided to address it as you propose.

Project Benefit

Describe the people, groups, and/or places expected to benefit from the project, and the ways they would benefit. Include demographic information (e.g., number, ethnicity, age, income levels, geographic area, etc.) for beneficiaries.

Project Effects

Outline the effects of the proposed project by providing a series of before and after snapshots in the spaces below. In each box on the left, briefly summarize existing conditions for that category. On the right, briefly describe the changed circumstances after the grant period has ended. Please give specific numbers and projections where appropriate. If a category does not apply, write NA.

Project Effects Chart

Before	After
Effect on organization's size, FTE, structure	
Effect on organization's programs	
Effect on organization's operating expenses	
Effect on organization's ability to generate income	
Effect on the issue or need project addresses	

Project Evaluation

Describe how the project's effectiveness will be determined.

Personnel Qualifications

Describe the qualifications and experience of people involved in implementing the project.

Lessons: This foundation's evaluation requirement isn't very detailed, nevertheless they look for the elements of a good evaluation plan:

- The needs statement should include baseline information for your clients or community in order to show changes in the outcomes.

- They want measurable outcomes, the results of their grant funding.

- They want projects that are well thought out, including the steps you would take to achieve outcomes, which a logic model would help describe.

- They want to know how you are going to capture information and learn from it, which is going to require some evaluation tools— maybe looking at records, maybe interviewing clients.

- The Martin Foundation's Project Effects Chart (shown at left) is designed to look at organizational and community impact, but it has some elements in common with a logic model. What's really interesting about it is that it looks at the applicant's whole organization, not just the project.

Based on this information, when planning a proposal to this funder, I would think about how I was going to do evaluation (discussed further in chapter 7). Keeping in mind their requirement to "describe how the project's effectiveness will be determined," I would focus on outcomes rather than statistics. I would think about how to integrate or coordinate the evaluation narrative with the Project Effects Chart and show outcomes not only for the client group but for the whole organization. I wouldn't be afraid to budget a small amount (3–5 percent) to evaluation and would describe what it would pay for, things such as interviews, focus groups, and analysis.

Templin Foundation

Interview: When I interviewed this program officer, I asked about the following:

- Why their foundation's application guidelines didn't include anything about evaluation or goals and objectives, but their reporting guidelines did. She said it had just never been a problem, that most applicants generally include goals and objectives in a proposal as a matter of course. Their more detailed reporting guidelines grew out of grantees asking what they wanted to see in reports. She said small service providers who don't get government funds and faith-based organizations often haven't had to think about outcomes or measurement before.

- If she wanted to see an evaluation section in proposals. She said it was a great benefit and provided a good basis for site visit questions.

- If she recommended logic models. She said they didn't see many of them, but they were helpful to pull out project specifics in a complex program.

- If they looked for best practices or evidence-based practices. She said it helps when it's clear applicants are aware of best practices in their field, that mentioning them strengthens a proposal. If they're trying a new program, what evidence do they have it will succeed?

- What she looks for in goals and objectives. She said measurable outcomes: if they're not clear at the beginning of a project, it's hard for an agency to know if their program makes a difference at the end. Are the goals in line with the organization's mission? She wants to know project effects on program effectiveness, program quality, and in the community.

Templin Foundation Grant Guidelines: This foundation's online grant submission guidelines have very little detail and don't even mention evaluation. They ask for "a narrative proposal describing the applicant organization, the project for which funds are sought, the persons to be served, and the number of persons affected."

However, the foundation's Grant Report Guidelines, on a different page of the site, ask much more probing questions:

Reports should answer the following questions:

1. What were the objectives for which the grant was requested, and what were the activities you undertook, or are undertaking, to meet these objectives?

2. Did your organization meet the goals set forth in the original grant proposal? Please explain.

3. As the project or program progressed, what modifications, if any, were made?

4. What has been the measurable effect of this project or program on your organization? For example, has it (1) helped to attract new private funding; (2) increased collaboration with other organizations; (3) increased volunteer involvement?

5. What has been the measurable effect of this project or program on the population you serve?

The Templin Foundation's questions are probably somewhat typical of family foundations that make awards in a particular state. Their giving is generous and thoughtful, but their process is still informal. They are well known in their region, and most of their grantees know the basics of grantwriting, so the foundation still gets proposals with needs statements, goals and objectives, timelines, and informal evaluation sections, without asking for them specifically.

Lessons: One lesson is to go beyond the basics in your research. For example, if you go to the Templin Foundation's Website and only look at the Submission Guidelines page, you get eligibility information and the one-sentence instruction asking for a narrative proposal. But if you go to the Grant Report Guidelines page, you get the five detailed questions shown above, which will help inform your planning and evaluation section. Explore the entire Website of any foundation you are researching.

As with the Martin Foundation application, I would include some evaluation planning in my project design. In addition to goals and objectives, I would think about program activities. In thinking about outcomes, I would go beyond the impact on clients and look at the organization's role in the community (collaboration, volunteers). As with the Martin Foundation, I would consider creating a logic model to show the relationships among resources, activities, outputs, outcomes, and impacts. I would demonstrate that I was aware of any research or best practices in the field.

I probably wouldn't budget for evaluation in a proposal to this funder. Their informality and direct service orientation would argue for a simple evaluation model (see chapter 1). If I were proposing a large program to multiple foundations, I would target any evaluation budget to one of the other, larger funders.

Cowles Foundation

Narrative Outline: This larger foundation can be more explicit about their evaluation requirements. The following example is taken from their narrative outline.

Project Description

- Present a detailed project overview including activities, timetable, who and how many benefit from the project, and how it meets the foundation's funding objectives.

- Document a compelling need for the project.

- Explain why the project is important for your organization and the community.

Qualifications

- Explain why your organization is appropriate to conduct the project, including identification of key personnel, their qualifications, and their roles in the project.

- Show how collaboration with others in your community, if applicable, will strengthen, extend, or otherwise be a factor in this project.

Results and Follow-Up

- Describe expected outcomes of the project and why its activities are expected to achieve these outcomes.

- Present plans for evaluating the effectiveness of the project.

- Describe the future funding plan, if applicable, to sustain the project after the grant period.

The challenge with the Cowles Foundation is that their narrative outline has a three-page limit. I would want to spend most of it on the project description and tie the outcomes back to the project overview. The plans for evaluation (Results and Follow-Up) would be briefly outlined, saying who would be involved and how the evaluation would document the outcomes.

Thurston Foundation

The Thurston Foundation is a general purpose foundation with a focus on higher education and research. Below are two sections from the foundation's very detailed guidelines:

Section L. Evaluation Plan: Describe how you will evaluate the progress and ultimate success of your project. In Section M you will state objectives. How will you determine or measure the extent to which these objectives have been reached? How will you determine if the project has been important to others, as discussed in Section I? Who will do the evaluation? What are the qualifications of those conducting the evaluation?

Section M. Your Plan and Expected Results: Describe how you will organize, staff, and move forward in order to address this problem or opportunity. Clearly state your measurable objectives in this project. Discuss the support and involvement of your Board. To what extent will you collaborate or cooperate with others and who are they? Estimate how many of your constituency will be affected by this project. Outline any pertinent timetable. In what ways will your solution and plan be both effective and creative? What are the expected outcomes of this project? Justify your budget and comment on your assumptions that costs are realistic.

The Thurston foundation is research oriented, so you could propose a formal evaluation to them. As you might expect, their staff will be thorough in looking at your proposal, so be sure the groundwork for the evaluation was carefully laid and that it furthered the project.

Foundations that Use a Common Grant Application

The National Network of Grantmakers is a collaborative of about 60 liberal and progressive social justice funders, mostly small- to medium-sized foundations, that have developed a common grant application form. There's not much focus on narrow project outcomes here. When applying to one of these foundations, tie the program outcomes into the societal impact and maybe team up with a university to get grad students to do an evaluation of your project's contribution to social change.

Following is a part of this application form that will help you design your evaluation section.

B. Describe your request (incorporating the following points:)

1. Problem statement: what problems, needs or issues does it address?

2. If other than general operating support, describe the program for which you seek funding, why you decided to pursue this project and whether it is a new or ongoing part of your organization.

3. What are the goals, objectives and activities/strategies involved in this request? Describe your specific activities/strategies using a timeline over the course of this request.

4. How does your work promote diversity and address inequality, oppression and discrimination within your organization as well as the larger society?

5. Describe systemic or social change you are trying to achieve: How does your work address and change the underlying or root causes of the problem?

GEO Due Diligence Tool

Grantmakers for Effective Organizations (GEO) is an organization of foundations interested in building strong and effective nonprofit organizations. GEO publishes the Due Diligence Tool[3] for use by funders in evaluating nonprofits and grants. Many foundations use it as presented or adapt it to their needs. The Organizational Vision and Strategy section and the Planning, Outcomes and Evaluation section of the tool contains the kinds of questions you need to anticipate and your executive director or board president should be prepared to answer, particularly when applying for a large, multiyear grant.

Organizational Vision and Strategy

The Organizational Vision section of the GEO Due Diligence Tool shows how funders are increasingly looking at the grant applicant's capability when making funding decisions. This is important because your proposal planning for major grants should grow out of your mission and strategic plan. Notice the questions about incorporating strategies into your work and keeping abreast of the latest thinking in your field. These tie directly into the research and best practices questions in the Project Planning section.

Although this chart is intended for foundations as an interviewing tool, it is invaluable as a model containing a series of questions a grantwriter can use in developing a narrative. It can also be used to help convince a reluctant executive director or board member of the importance of strategic planning and evaluation to successful grants.

---

[3] The GEO Due Diligence Tool can be downloaded free from http://www.geofunders.org.

GEO—Organizational Vision and Strategy

Setting the vision and overall direction of the organization is a key role for the board to undertake. Working in partnership with the executive director and other staff leadership, the board must engage in developing strategy and plans for the organization. This involves having a strong understanding of the environment in which the organization is working. Visioning and strategy formation require an important blend of governance and leadership that warrants special attention in due diligence, as it is so critical to a successful organization.

Interviewees: Executive director, board chair and/or other board member(s)

Figure 6-1. GEO Organizational Vision and Strategy

Category of Issues	Questions to Consider	Indictors of Effectiveness	Red Flags
Vision	What is your organization's mission? What is your vision for the organization?	Agreement between E.D. and board as to the mission and long-term vision for the organization.	Leadership is unable to articulate mission and/or vision.
Strategy Formation	How do you set overall direction for the organization? Do you have a current strategic plan? If not, how do you develop strategy? Who is involved in the strategic planning and thinking? How do you incorporate current strategies into your work?	A current strategy for achieving the organization's mission with realistic goals. Involvement of the board in strategy development.	Leadership cannot describe any internal process by which opportunities are evaluated and/or goals are set.
External Environment	How does the organization keep abreast of the latest thinking in your field? What are the top three challenges facing the organization over the next five years?	Leadership can describe programmatic trends or movements in the field and how they will affect the organization's work.	Inability to articulate major challenges beyond needing funds.

Planning, Outcomes, and Evaluation Chart

Another useful section of the GEO Due Diligence Tool deals with your organization's proposed project planning, outcomes, and evaluation. Below is part of the Proposed Project section of the tool:

GEO—Proposed Project: Planning, Outcomes and Evaluation

Your initial proposal review should have given you a good sense of the project that the applicant seeks to implement. The written word, however, has its limits. Having a conversation with the applicant is a key step in going deeper in your understanding of what the leaders seek to accomplish.

In your conversation, ask the applicant about the approach and plan for the project, as well as the resources needed to implement it. You should also focus on the programmatic goals and outcomes the applicant has established, ensuring they are well defined, meaningful, and measurable.

Evaluation has several purposes. Engaging in ongoing evaluation provides organizations with information about moving toward success in achieving outcomes and provides guidance regarding what's working and what needs to be changed and improved. Evaluation also provides knowledge for the benefit of others in the field, both practitioners and funders. Finally, sound evaluation practices help to ensure accountability.

Most grantmakers require some form of program evaluation from at least some of their (larger) grantees, though the depth and focus can vary widely. Although formal evaluation is generally prohibitively expensive for grantees, effective organizations should be able to articulate intended outcomes and describe a plan for tracking and measuring the success of their work. They should have methods of measuring their impact and incorporating what they learn into their program practices.

For some grantmakers, a grantee's lack of capacity to track and measure its work is a "deal breaker." For others, because that capacity is very important, there is a commitment of resources to work with grantees to build it. Because evaluation is expensive, grantmakers that require outside evaluation generally provide the funds to support the work. Other funders seek only basic monitoring and assessment, which can be handled in-house by the grantee. So, the key issue is whether you are getting the evaluation information necessary to match your particular institution's values and standards.

Interviewees: Executive director, key program staff, board member that is a project "champion" or supporter

Figure 6-2. GEO Planning, Outcomes, and Evaluation Chart

Category of Issues	Questions to Consider	Indictors of Effectiveness	Red Flags
Project Planning	Describe the basis for your approach to this project. What research do you rely upon for your proposed approach? Describe the resources needed to accomplish your goals, and how you plan to obtain them. If relevant, discuss the following: • Scalability of model • Replicability of model • Potential for broad impact • An innovative approach	Methodology makes sense, given what is considered accepted or best practice in the field. Project design supports the applicant's theory of change (whether consciously articulated or implicit). Project plan allocates appropriate resources (staff, expertise, money, an appropriate time frame) to accomplish what is anticipated.	Logic model or rationale for the program does not make sense. Approach is outmoded, showing a lack of awareness of developments in the field in recent years.
Project Outcomes	What are the goals and outcomes identified for the project? What was the process for developing the outcomes? How do you use lessons learned from previous years or projects? Describe your organization's greatest strengths in terms of your capacity to achieve its intended outcomes. What significant challenges exist in your capacity to achieve your intended outcomes?	Desired outcomes are plausible and aligned with nonprofit's mission and strategy. Goals are realistic and achievable within the grant period. Resources available are appropriate, and the cost of the program will result in a reasonable impact. Outcomes are SMART: Specific, Measurable, Achievable, Realistic, and Time sensitive.	Project plans are overreaching: Goals are too ambitious or resources available are clearly insufficient to reach the goals. Outcomes are not in alignment with the theory of change for the project. Cost-benefit analysis is unacceptable (i.e., it is not worth the expense for the anticipated impact).
Evaluation	How do you evaluate your programs? What tools do you have in place? How do you incorporate what you learn into your ongoing and future work? What is the plan for evaluation of this project? What resources are allocated for evaluation in the project budget?	Organization knows what it accomplishes and can articulate how it will apply what it learns. If outcomes are not achieved, leaders can explain why and have strategies to improve ability to meet outcomes.	Organization has no understanding of the value of tracking its outcomes.

Government Agencies

Federal—and most local—government social service grants are entirely different from those of foundations. It's generally very clear that they want an extensive evaluation section, because they spell it out in extensive detail in the Request for Proposal (RFP). The problem is often getting through the bureaucratic writing style to determine exactly what they're trying to say. It would be clear to me on reading the RFP presented below that most nonprofit organizations would want to contract with an experienced outside evaluator to help develop the program and write the evaluation section of this proposal (and see chapter 2).

Evaluation Questions in a Typical Government RFP

Below is a fairly typical RFP[4] evaluation section from CSAT, the Center for Substance Abuse Treatment (which is part of SAMHSA, the Substance Abuse and Mental Health Services Administration). If you're not familiar with federal RFPs, know that this is taken from a 64-page document, which also includes a 17-page Client Outcome Measures data collection instrument to use in collecting and recording client information.

As you read this excerpt, take note of the following points:

- The first section (2.7) gives background on why they're doing the evaluation, lists performance measures, says they require use of the Client Outcome Measures data collection tool mentioned above, specifies that you collect individual baseline data, and offers training in data collection.

- The next section (2.8) says they'll require both process and outcome evaluation. They won't require comparison groups, and they limit evaluation to 20 percent of the budget. (This means that you should plan on spending at least 15 percent to be taken seriously.)

- The third piece (Section D) gives instructions for writing the evalua-tion section. This proposal has 100 possible points, which is typical; evaluation counts for 15 points.

---

[4] RFA No. TI-06-004. *Projects to Deliver and Evaluate Peer-to-Peer Recovery Support Services; Short Title: Recovery Community Services Program, RCSP.* (CFDA) No. 93.243.

2.7 Data and Performance Measurement

Performance Measurement: All SAMHSA grantees are required to collect and report certain data so that SAMHSA can meet its obligations under the Government Performance and Results Act (GPRA). Grantees will be required to report performance in several areas relating to the client's substance use, family and living conditions, employment status, social connectedness, access to treatment, retention in treatment and criminal justice status. This information will be gathered using the data collection tool referenced below. The collection of these data will enable CSAT to report on the National Outcome Measures (NOMs), which have been defined by SAMHSA as key priority areas relating to substance use.

The purpose of the RCSP GPRA data is to provide information that helps to establish the value of peer-to-peer recovery support services in preventing relapse and promoting sustained recovery. To accomplish this, you will be required to provide data on a set of required performance indicators.

For adults and adolescents/youth receiving services, GPRA indicators include changes in a positive direction or stability over time on each of the following measures, showing that participants receiving your services:

- Have not used illegal drugs or misused alcohol or prescription drugs during the past month.
- Are currently employed or engaged in productive activities.
- Have reduced their involvement with the criminal justice system.
- Have a permanent place to live in the community.
- Have increased or maintained positive social connections.
- Have experienced increased access to recovery support and other services.
- Are being retained in your program.

Please note: Although SAMHSA recognizes the important role that family members and significant others can play in supporting an individual's recovery, the GPRA tool is not appropriate for family members or others who are not themselves in recovery. Therefore, although you may propose activities and services for family members, you should not plan to conduct GPRA performance data collection and reporting for individuals who are not personally in recovery from substance use disorders.

Applicants must document their ability to collect and report the required data in "Section D: Evaluation and Data" of their applications. You should not, however, include GPRA data collection forms. If you do not have the capability to collect and report on the GPRA measures, you will need to partner with an individual or organization that does.

Grantees must collect and report data using the Discretionary Services Client Level GPRA tool, which can be found at www.samhsa-gpra.samhsa.gov (click on CSAT-GPRA, then click on "Data Collection Tools/Instructions"), along with instructions for completing it. Hard copies are available in the application kits distributed by SAMHSA's National Clearinghouse for Alcohol and Drug Information.

GPRA data must be collected at baseline (i.e., the client's entry into the project), discharge, and 6 months after the baseline. After GPRA data are collected, data must then be entered into CSAT's GPRA Data Entry and Reporting System (www.samhsa-gpra.samhsa.gov) within 7 business days of the forms being completed. In addition, 80% of the participants must be followed up.

Training and technical assistance on data collecting, tracking, and follow-up, as well as data entry, will be provided by CSAT.

The terms and conditions of the grant award also will specify the data to be submitted and the schedule for submission. Grantees will be required to adhere to these terms and conditions of award.

2.8 Evaluation

Grantees must evaluate their projects, and you are required to describe your evaluation plans in your application. The evaluation should be designed to provide regular feedback to the project to improve services. The evaluation must include the required GPRA performance measures (outcome evaluation) described above, as well as process components (process evaluation—described below), which measure change relating to project goals and objectives over time compared to baseline information. Control or comparison groups are not required.

Process components should address issues such as:

- How closely did implementation match the plan?

- What types of deviation from the plan occurred?

- What led to the deviations?

- What effect did the deviations have on the planned intervention and evaluation?

- Who provided (program staff, peer leaders) what services (modality, type, intensity, duration), to whom (individual characteristics), in what context (organization, community), and at what cost (facilities, personnel, dollars)?

You may use no more than 20% of the total grant award for evaluation and data collection, including GPRA.

Section D: Evaluation and Data (15 points)

- Document your ability to collect, manage, and report on the required performance measures as explained in Section I-2.7 of this RFA. (Note: It is not necessary to include any performance measures other than those listed in Section I-2.7 in your evaluation design. SAMHSA/CSAT will provide the necessary protocols and forms for collection and reporting of data on these measures, so you do not need to include data collection forms for these measures in your application.)

- If you choose to collect data on any performance measures in addition to those identified in Section I-2.7, you must specify and justify the additional measures. If you choose to include additional performance measures in your outcome evaluation, you must also describe your plans for data collection, management, analysis, interpretation, and reporting. You must also include your valid and reliable data collection instruments in Appendix 2.

- Describe the process evaluation and explain how it will reflect the experience and lessons learned from your project. Include in Appendix 2 any forms or protocols you plan to use for your process evaluation.

Coordinating Grant and Evaluation Planning | 7

MOST GRANTWRITERS APPROACH EVALUATION as one section of a proposal, to be done toward the end of grant development. However, I believe it will greatly improve both your planning and the final proposal to think about evaluation from the beginning and to include it in your entire grant planning process. In addition, the sooner you can decide on the type of evaluation to do and identify the evaluator, the more help they can be in designing your whole project. Figure 7-1 outlines a step-by-step approach to incorporating evaluation into the planning and writing of major grant proposals.

Read the Guidelines

As you start work on a major grant project, one of the first steps is reading over the funder's guidelines or request for proposals (RFP). If it sets requirements for evaluation, you have an automatic starting place for planning your evaluation. In some cases an RFP will require that a certain percent of a grant be spent on evaluation, which will help you to budget. However, keep in mind that the funder's requirements are a minimum and not a limitation on how you can use the evaluation. Could this evaluation's results begin defining your program as an evidence-based practice? Would a strong formative evaluation help with organizational or management improvements your organization is planning? In other words, the required evaluation component can actually be structured to meet your needs as well as those of the funders.

An opposite situation may occur with local family foundations, which may want all of their grant dollars to go to direct services. I've had grants staff react in horror that an applicant wanted to spend their money on evaluation. In these cases, decide if doing minimum data collection for reporting is adequate to your organization's needs, or if the project is such that you want to design a no-cost evaluation, or if you even want to look for separate evaluation funding.

Figure 7-1. Coordinating Grant and Evaluation Planning

Grant	Evaluation
RFP or Guidelines	**Funder requirements for evaluation**
Organizational Description • Capability, qualifications • Mission • Current programs • History • Strategic plan	Understand the environment • Political issues, financial limitations affecting evaluation • Type and scale of evaluation • In-house or outside evaluator?
Needs Statement • Community description • Client or participant description • Information gathering	Information gathering • Baseline data • Literature review • Secondary data
Goals and Objectives • SMART • Related to needs statement • Answers the questions, Who?, What?, When?, Where?, Why?, How?	Evaluation design • SMART • Set benchmarks; decide what to evaluate • Methodology (QUAN, QUAL, or mixed?) • Decide what data to gather • Methods of gathering data (instruments) • Sources of information
Logic Model	
Narrative and procedures • Approach • Work plan	Formative evaluation • Is the theory being followed? • Method for feedback and improvement Summative evaluation • Plan for collecting and analyzing data
Timeline	Evaluation timeline • Longitudinal evaluation • Choosing control groups • Pre- and post-program testing • Data collection schedule • Report schedule
Evaluation	Write evaluation section
Sustainability	Does evaluation support continuation of this program?
Personnel qualifications	Staff doing evaluation Outside evaluator
Replication and dissemination	Evaluation report and documentation

Compose the Organizational Description

As you work on the organizational description or capability statement, think about the evaluation needs of your organization. Every major grant should be congruent with your agency's mission and fit into your strategic plan, if you have one. Are there ways a good program evaluation would strengthen your organization's standing in the community? Are there political issues, internal or external, that need to be considered in planning the evaluation? This is the time to start thinking about the type and scale of the evaluation, and whether to do it in-house or use an outside evaluator. For instance, if your organization has had credibility issues, an independent evaluation by a local university may help mend your reputation.

Research the Needs Statement

This is the first place where the work of developing the grant proposal and the work of designing the program evaluation come together. In fact, a needs assessment is sometimes called a preliminary evaluation. As you research community and client needs for the grant proposal, you are also gathering baseline data that can be used for your evaluation. You may begin by looking at your own agency files to document client needs. Thinking about what data you need for your evaluation may expose missing pieces or weaknesses in your recordkeeping, which could help improve your case management. You can also document your organization's successes in working with the target population.

In addition to your own records, you will probably look for research and statistics that show the need for your program. Federal, state, and local government agencies often have statistical studies and reports that will document problems. In most cases you'll want to make the case locally, while showing that you know what's going on nationally in the field. Data and statistics from governments, universities, academic journals, and online sources is called secondary data because it's not from your own sources.

If you're planning a major evaluation, this is a good time to do a literature review. Although not included in most grant need statements, a lit review adds an impressive framework to your proposal. If you're working with an outside evaluator who is familiar with your program area, often they will be knowledgeable about the current literature in the field and can do the literature review for you.

Define the Goals and Objectives

As you begin describing the actual program for which you're seeking funding, you need to define the program's goals and objectives. The convention in grantwriting is that *goals* are broad descriptions of what you want to accomplish, while *objectives* are quantifiable results of the project. Many people describe objectives as being SMART: Specific, Measurable, Achievable, Realistic, and Time-limited. Evaluation raises the question of "SMART as measured by what?", requiring us to look closely at each of our objectives.

As you write each objective, draft an evaluation measure. This may help you to refine and improve your objectives, thereby strengthening your proposal. Then decide what information you need to collect to measure the objective, data sources, and timeline.

In an article on the online CharityChannel *Grants and Foundation Review*, Maryn Boess proposes a fill-in-the-blanks model for developing SMART objectives.[5] It includes: Time frame, Intervention, What portion of what target group, Direction of change, Area of impact, Degree of impact, Measured by what indicators, Using what indicators, and Administered when.

In this excerpt from the article, Maryn takes a literacy program with the vague outcome statement "to help participants improve their reading skills" and runs it through her model:

> Remember our initial success indicator: "To help participants improve their reading skills"? How do we get from this 98-pound weakling to a powerhouse outcome statement that wins friends and influences funders? Time to introduce the fill-in-the-blanks model suggested by my colleague Sandra Simmons. Starting with your skinny little success indicator, think through each of the following questions about your vision of the change you intend to create. (We've filled in the blanks with our literacy example.)
>
> - Time frame: (By what date? Within what time period?) After six months . . .
>
> - Intervention: (What is the work or service you're applying to create the intended change?) . . . of one-on-one tutoring . . .
>
> - What portion of what target group: . . . 75% of the adult learners served by this project . . .
>
> - Direction of change: (Is something going up or down, getting larger or smaller?) . . . will improve . . .

[5] "SMART? Targets: A Fill-in-the-Blanks Model for Crafting Unbeatable Outcome Measures." Wednesday, February 9, 2005. http://charitychannel.com/enewsletters/gfr/

- Area of impact: (What is going up or down, getting larger or smaller?) . . . their reading skills . . .
- Degree of impact: . . . by two grade levels . . .
- As measured by what indicators: . . . as measured by their scores . . .
- Using what instrument: . . . on the Lumbard Literacy Evaluation Scale . . .
- Administered when: . . . administered at the beginning and end of the six-month period.

Put all the fill-ins together, and here's what you get:

"After six months of one-on-one tutoring, 75% of the adult learners served by this project will improve their reading skills by two grade levels, as measured by their scores on the Lumbard Literacy Evaluation Scale administered at the beginning and end of the six-month period."

Voila! A fool-proof outcome measure that will inspire confidence in your funders every time.

The process of developing goals and objectives is the real beginning of your evaluation design. It is where you decide what you're going to evaluate, what data you'll need to collect, and how and from where you'll gather the data. You need to have the evaluator involved in this stage, whether it's someone inside your organization or an outside consultant.

A final thought on goals and objectives. Including evaluation as a program objective with its own activities and measurable outcomes shows the reader that you're serious about evaluation and integrating it into your project.

Using Logic Models

For many grant proposals, the goals and objectives will be the basis for describing your program theory and developing a logic model. A logic model shows how you can tie the components of your grant proposal together. We'll look at logic models in depth in the next chapter.

Narrative and Procedures

Along with the goals and objectives, you will be writing the narrative description of your grant proposal. This describes the approach you'll take and sets out a work plan for accomplishing the goals and objectives. The narrative is the major writing section of most grants.

As you organize your work for writing the narrative, you can think about how you would document and demonstrate your work. For a process evaluation, this is where you ask the question, "How will we know the theory and project described is being followed?" In a formative evaluation, this is where you'd decide on methods for feedback from the evaluation and program improvements.

Timelines

In most major proposals you develop a timeline for hiring staff, carrying out the program, and reaching milestones. Alongside this timeline you can be developing an evaluation timeline. If you'll use control groups, when will they be selected? If you plan on doing pre- and post-program tests of participants, when will they be administered? When will you collect data, and when will you deliver program reports? For a longitudinal evaluation, how will you track participants through time, possibly including after the grant funded project formally ends?

Evaluation

If you've done the work above, the evaluation section will practically write itself, and you'll have a better proposal to boot.

Sustainability

This section generally asks how you will fund program continuation after grant funding ends. Evaluation will provide you with information about whether the program should be continued in its present form. If the answer is positive, the evaluation report will provide you with ammunition to seek continuation funding.

Personnel

Along with the usual program and administrative staff qualifications, you should include information on the evaluator, whether it's someone on your staff or an outside contractor.

Replication and Dissemination

For many major grants, especially federal ones, the funder wants to know if your program can be replicated by others. In other cases, they want to know if and how you will disseminate the results of your grant-funded project to the world. Your final evaluation report and supporting data will give you the material for either or both of these purposes, as appropriate.

Logic Models and Theory of Change | 8

THE LOGIC MODEL is evaluation's gift to grantwriters. These simple diagrams visually show how your grant program does its work. It's a tool you can use with staff in developing a grant proposal, a graphic for showing a funder how its grant will work with other resources to make community change, and a framework for designing your evaluation. Talk about a picture being worth a thousand words!

Although the practice of diagramming programs was used as early as the 1970s, program logic models first became widely used in the 1990s as part of theory-based evaluation. *Theory-based evaluation* says that every social program has a program theory that explains how it works, even if it is not well suited to statistical analysis of its outcomes. However, the theory is often implicit and unstated, with program staff unaware or even denying that they work from a theory. Program theory is a way of identifying people's assumptions about resources and activities, and how they lead to intended outcomes. It allows us to think about causality—Did this program actually cause these results?—in the absence of statistical proof. The logic model is a tool for describing the program theory.

When you get program managers and line staff together to talk about a grant proposal, they may collectively know what their program's goals are, while they have different individual ideas of how it works. The work of developing a logic model can get everyone on the same page and moving in the same direction. They can set goals and priorities, decide what needs to be measured, and work out differences. The program's theory of change will emerge, which may help them conceptualize their work.

Sample Logic Model

Let's look at a commonly used logic model and its component pieces. There are different kinds, but one of the most common is an *outcome logic model*, shown in Figure 8-1.

Figure 8-1. Logic Model Components with Examples

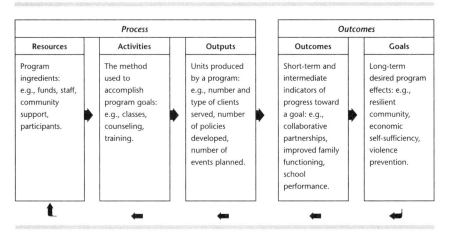

© 1995 The Evaluation Forum. Used with permission.

Each component is linked to the next in a conditional logic (if–then) relationship, like computer programming in Basic. IF you have access to resources, THEN you can carry out program activities. IF you carry out program activities, THEN you can deliver program services (outputs). IF you provide program services, THEN clients will benefit (outcomes). IF your clients benefit, THEN hoped-for changes will happen in your community (goals). The arrows across the bottom show feedback from a formative evaluation, which is used to make program improvements.

- **Resources** are the program inputs, the ingredients that support and undergird your program. They are people or things: staff, funding, clients, facilities, curricula, program manuals, technology, consultants, partner organizations.

- **Activities** are the methods used to deliver your program, either processes or events: counseling, training, case management, classes, community forums, recreational opportunities.

- **Outputs** are service units, the direct and measurable products of your program's activities: number of clients served or classes held.

- **Outcomes** are the results or impact of the activities: increased school attendance, improved grades, stable employment, safe housing, mental health stability.

- **Goals** are the long-term changes you want your program to make. They connect your program to your organization's mission and provide direction and focus for the program: violence prevention, child abuse prevention, access to health care, reduction in criminal behavior.

To see how this works, let's look at a multilevel violence prevention program. The theory behind this early intervention program is that intervening with children and their families can reduce violent behavior. It offers graduated levels of intensity, providing basic education to all of the children in the school, with increasing levels of training and counseling for higher-risk youth. Because these are young schoolchildren, outcomes would probably be tracked through teacher and parent observation and reporting. The proof will be whether program participants show reductions in these problem behaviors at the end of the grant period. The school might want to follow the children through later grades and see if the good behavior continued. Figure 8-2 shows a program logic model for such a program.

Figure 8-2. Program Logic Model for a School and Community
Violence Prevention Project

Process				Outcomes	
Resources	Activities	Outputs		Outcomes	Goals
• Staff	• Delivery of violence prevention curriculum in the schools (pre-K to 4th grade)	• 4–6 hours of violence prevention education for 1,890 students (pre-K to 4th grade)		• Improvement in healthy peer social communica- tion	• Violence Prevention
• Violence prevention curriculum					
• Case management services	• Intensive violence prevention groups to high-risk youth	• 480 students receive intensive prevention training in ten groups of 6–10 students each		• Reduction in violent behaviors in school	
• Partnerships: university, counseling centers, sheriff's department, school district	• Intensive outreach services to families with high-risk youth	• 185 at-risk families receive intensive outreach services		• Increase in healthy behavioral patterns in handling stress	
• Participants	• DARE (Drug Abuse Resistance Education)	• 60 at-risk families receive Family Empowerment Project services		• Improved school-related behaviors	
	• Family Empowerment Project services to families			• Increase in family support	
				• Customer satisfaction	

© 1995 The Evaluation Forum. Used with permission.

Developing a Logic Model and Program Theory

Whereas there are many approaches to developing program theories, for the purposes of grant development, most writers advise starting from the right side of the logic model chart at Goals and working backward to Resources. This path can give you greater flexibility and help break down preconceptions that might be missed when working in the usual left-to-right direction.

To begin, have a meeting of the people involved with your grant proposal, including the ultimate decision makers. These could include the program director, executive director, the program staff who would be working in the project, financial manager, evaluator, and grantwriter. Start with a blank chart set up like the one in Figure 8-3 below. Print out several one-page copies for participants to use, and draw one on a flip chart for the group's use. The figure includes some questions you can use to move the process along.

Figure 8-3. Sample Interview Questions for Building a Program Logic Model

Process			Outcomes	
Resources	Activities	Outputs	Outcomes	Goals
What do we need to make this program succeed?	What do we need to accomplish?	What will these activities produce that we can measure?	What changes will result from these activities?	What are the desired long-term impacts of this program?
Who in your organization will be involved? Where will this happen? What other partners or collaborators will be needed? Who is your client population? What strengths do they bring to the program? What are the necessary materials, curricula, transportation, etc., for this program?	What activities occur within each major program component? Is the program based on best practices or other models?	How many clients or participants will you serve? Who are they? How many processes, client contacts, events will take place? What objectives have you set for this program? What are the RFP or contract performance requirements (if any)?	What changes in behavior, knowledge, or attitude would you expect to see at the end of this program? How will you identify and measure these changes?	What change(s) do you want to create with this program? What does success look like in the community? How will clients' lives be different?

© 1995 The Evaluation Forum. Used with permission.

1. **Goals:** What is the impact your organization would like this program to make in the community? If people have different visions, they need to agree on goals before meaningful outcomes can be decided.

2. **Outcomes:** This is where things start to get specific. What measurable indictors do you want to use to gauge success in meeting the program goals? You might have two to five outcomes for each goal. If appropriate, these can be broken into short-term (1–3 years) and long-term (4+ years) indicators.

3. **Outputs:** Now you start to quantify things. How many participants will be affected? How many classes will be held, or trees planted? How many people will find jobs, or housing, or attend concerts?

4. **Activities:** What program activities or services need to be conducted to achieve the outputs and outcomes?

5. **Resources:** Think about all of the things that needed to implement each activity. Personnel, equipment and supplies, travel, participants, community partners, funding, and so forth.

6. **Program Theory:** If your group didn't have an articulated program theory when they started (which is likely), now you're ready to develop one. Remember the if–then sequential relationships above? The program theory fits into the logic model between the Outputs and Outcomes boxes. What does the group believe is the relationship between the Process section and the Outcomes section? The formula is IF (Resources, Activities, Outputs) – THEN (Outcomes, Goals). If everyone can agree on the program theory, you've created buy-in for the program.

7. **Review:** Go back through the model from left to right, Resources to Goals. Are any steps or key resources missing? Put the outcomes in sequential order and check your reasoning. Look for unsupported assumptions or missing data.

8. **Refine:** Get feedback on the logic model from stakeholders. Depending on the project this could include the executive director (if they weren't in the group), board of directors, the funder, clients, or community partners. If someone will be crucial to the success of the program, or highly impacted by it, this is a chance to get their input.

This will probably be as far as you go in most cases, at least with the whole group. If you're working with an outside evaluator, he or she may want to work through more detailed versions of the model to determine what data will be needed for the evaluation. You may meet with the program director to determine staff and budget needs for the project and make sure it's realistic and achievable.

One proviso: Before you begin work on developing the program logic model, it's vitally important to have defined the need for the program and the problem to be solved. In many cases, the grantwriter will be called into a meeting to discuss a grant project with a looming RFP deadline and not have had time to write the proposal's needs statement. The program staff may have a clear idea of the problem, even if they don't have documentation at hand. The group needs to get general agreement on the problem and need before starting work on the logic model.

Goals and Objectives vs. Outputs and Outcomes

Grant guidelines from foundations and government agencies often ask for your program's goals and objectives. However, the program logic model talks about outputs and outcomes. They are similar, so it's important to note the differences when developing your proposal.

- **Goals** are broad descriptions of what you want your program to accomplish (some evaluators call them *program impacts*.)

- **Objectives** are the details, the quantifiable subsets of goals. Many people describe objectives as being SMART: Specific, Measurable, Achievable, Realistic, and Time-limited. They usually begin with an action verb and include key results.

- **Outcomes**, as noted above, are the results or impact of your program's activities. They are indicators that your program is having its intended effect. What will change in the lives of your clients or in the community as a result of your program? Although outcomes are measurable, they may or may not be numerically measurable because they are concerned with answering the question, So what?

- **Outputs** are service units, the direct and measurable products of your program's activities. They answer the questions, How many?, How often?, How long?, without talking about Why? or So what?

In writing your grant proposal, the goals from the logic model will generally serve for your goals and objectives section. However, objectives and outcomes can be different. Whereas objectives address the results of staff activities, outcomes focus on the impact on participants' lives of those staff activities. If you use a logic model exercise to develop your program, keep this difference in mind when you get to writing goals and objectives.

Types of Outcome Statements[6]

There are various types of outcome statements—different ways to describe what a program is striving to achieve:

- **Change Statements** include the increase, maintenance, or decrease in behavior, skill, knowledge, or attitude, etc.
  Example: Increase immunization among young children.

- **Target Statements** state specific levels of achievement.
  Example: Immunize 80 percent of two-year-old children in the community according to recommended public health schedules.

- **Benchmark Statements** include comparative targets, generally related to other time periods or organizations.
  Example: Increase the current 70 percent immunization rate for children aged 0 to 24 months to 90 percent by the year 2002.

Logic Model Pitfalls and How to Avoid Them

Time: Developing a logic model can be time consuming.

- Avoid trying for perfection.
- If necessary, leave some elements unknown.

Too linear: Real life often isn't linear, but people tend to assume things happen sequentially.

- Recognize that the linear model can be a helpful simplification.
- Use more complex models like a tree diagram or color-coding to show timing.

Too rigid: The model is not responsive to new information.

- Develop the model with staff and stakeholders.
- Revisit and revise the logic model during program implementation.

---

[6] Excerpts from *Outcomes for Success, The Evaluation Forum 2000*. Used with permission.

Program Logic Models for Grants

In using logic models for grant funding, you will find many versions, from the simple to the complex. Most program logic models will be variations of the one we've looked at, and most will come with their own instructions. Different federal agencies have their own versions, depending on their areas of interest.

There are many approaches to this subject, and some writers or organizations have different definitions and differing opinions on the relationship of logic models and theory of change. I recommend two sources for practical use in grant development. *Outcomes for Success!* by the Evaluation Forum presents a practical overview and a good workbook for logic model development. The *W. K. Kellogg Foundation Logic Model Development Guide* offers a more academic study of different kinds of logic models. Both are listed in the Bibliography.

Developing an Evaluation Plan | 9

ALTHOUGH THE LOGIC MODEL grew out of evaluation, it is actually more of a program design tool than an evaluation design tool. The logic model provides a structure for creating details (outputs, outcomes) out of program concepts. The theory of change looks at the program concepts and teases out the underlying assumptions.

We can use another similar looking tool, and Evaluation Planning Chart (Figure 9-1), to design your evaluation plan. Unlike the logic model, each piece does not follow logically from the previous one, but they are all related. When you used the logic model, you created expected outcomes. The program evaluation plan starts with these outcomes and decides the appropriate ways to measure whether the outcomes are being met.

For the logic model, you gathered together people directly involved in the program. For this exercise, the group is much smaller. The grantwriter, program director, and person who will be directing the evaluation may be all you need. If you're using a trained evaluator, either internal or an outside contractor, they may take this part on by themselves. If this is the case, you want to be involved at least enough to be able to write about it, and the program director will want to be involved enough to see how it will impact their staff and operations. You both may accomplish this by walking through a late draft of the plan with the evaluator, but be sure it's in time for you to have some input.

The first step is determining the purpose of your evaluation. Just like the program it studies, the evaluation should have an aim and stated goals. The grantwriter, program director, and evaluator may get together to discuss this before starting work on the evaluation plan. The purpose will help determine what you measure and how many resources you want to devote to the evaluation.

Next, identify the audience(s) and resources available for the evaluation. What does this audience want to know about your program's impact or efficiency? Is this to be a formative evaluation for program improvement or a summative evaluation to show that it worked? How much money is available to pay for the evaluation? Will you be using an experienced evaluator or regular program staff? How much time will staff be able to devote to collecting data? The necessary resources will be impacted by the number of program participants, frequency of observation, number of data collection instruments used and their complexity, length of time data will be collected, and availability of existing data.

Once you've made these decisions, you're ready to start planning. Figure 9-1 shows the topics to help you devise your evaluation plan, along with useful questions. As with the logic model exercise, have a blank form for each participant and a flipchart for group work.

Below are details about how to use the topics in the chart.

- **Outcomes:** Start with the outcomes from the logic model, which are the things you hope will happen as a result of your program. Each outcome gets its own box in the evaluation chart, which carries across the page to all the other categories.

- **Key Indicators:** Decide what you want to know about the outcomes. What factors would influence the outcomes? What could you measure as evidence of your outcomes being met? Phrase these so that they don't assume a direction (e.g., *change* in test scores, not *increase* in test scores), because your results may be different from your expectations. Remember that evidence could be quantitative or qualitative, and that you might want to measure either or both. Numeric terms such as "number of" directs you to quantitative methods, whereas "knowledge of" leads to qualitative measurement.

- **Sources of Information:** Where or from whom can you gather information? This could be people inside or outside your organization, including program participants. It could be case files, databases of program information, and/or numbers from government agencies that track your target population.

- **Methods:** In Sources you identified *where* you would gather information. Here you decide *how* you can best collect information from your sources. It could be quantifiable records (forms, document reviews, surveys, tests) that will tell you how much, how many, what percentage of change occurred. Methods can also be qualitative, exploring people's experiences, thoughts, and feelings about the program. Focus groups, interviews, and observations will help tell you why and how your program worked (or not), or whether some parts worked better than others.

Figure 9-1. Evaluation Planning Chart

Outcomes	Key Indicators	Sources of Information	Methods	Timeline	Responsibility
What parts of the program do we want to evaluate?	What can we measure or observe?	Where or from whom can we gather information?	How will we gather the information?	When does this need to be done?	Who will do it, or see that it gets done?
Written as change statements, targets, or benchmarks. Related to the organization's mission. Realistic and attainable by this program. They are something this program can actually impact.	Directly related to the outcome. Specific, measurable, and observable. Appropriate to the outcome being measured. Refrain from using directional or numeric terms.	*Internal*: Organization staff, program participants, case files, organization records, program database. *External*: Government agency reports, census data, participants' families, other agencies that work with participants (i.e., schools, parole departments).	Use off-the-shelf instruments or develop your own? Make sure instruments are valid, reliable, culturally appropriate, and realistic.	Activities before intervention (pre-test, baselines)? How frequently will you collect data? Are milestones or required interim reports required? How long will it take to analyze data? Will there be long-term follow-up after the program?	Program director, program staff, participants (diaries), evaluator, statistician, outside contractors.

- **Timeline:** You need to decide in advance when to gather information. Baseline data and pre-testing must be done before the project begins. Ongoing testing or surveys must be scheduled at specified times. Reports to funders or other groups may be due on particular dates. Remember to include time to train data collectors and pilot-test the collection process.

- **Responsibility:** Who is going to gather this information, interpret it, write reports, and so forth? Don't just list "program staff"; identify a person by name or job title. This will help you clarify staff and consultant roles if you're using an outside evaluator. If you're conducting the evaluation in-house, it helps you decide or assign responsibility within your staff.

After you have completed the evaluation plan, review it to ensure the concepts are clear and distinct. Verify that the indictors are really measurable. Go back to the goal(s) in your logic model, and be sure that the indicators and methods will measure the goals, and that nothing has been missed. Is all of the information in your plan necessary to judge the accomplishment of your goals? If not, remove any extra activities that would divert time and energy from the core evaluation.

Finally, remember that all of the information gathered will have to be organized, analyzed, interpreted, documented, and reported. Even if you have done most of the data collection in-house, you may want to consult with an experienced evaluator on this stage. Also remember that this will all take time, so allow some time either at the end of your grant period or after it for results to be available.

Writing Your Evaluation Section | 10

AFTER YOU'VE IDENTIFIED your type of evaluation, decided who's going to do it, drawn your logic model, and developed your evaluation plan, it's time to bite the bullet and write the evaluation section of your grant proposal. After doing all that groundwork, you know your subject, but how are you going to present it to your funder? Here are some tips for writing a dynamite evaluation section.[7]

1. Make it easy for the reviewers to confirm that your evaluation meets the criteria listed in the RFP. Use standard evaluation terminology; in fact, use the *funder's language* whenever appropriate. Resist the temptation to list complicated evaluation strategies or statistical methods that you don't understand or can't explain. If you say you will perform both formative and summative evaluations, explain in simple language how you will do that. Make it clear that you know what you're writing about and that your organization has the capacity to carry it out.

2. Relate your evaluation methods directly to your objectives and outcomes. If you have already developed a logic model and an evaluation plan, you have designed these relationships. In fact, you can include your evaluation plan chart to show how they all fit together, making sure it matches your narrative.

3. Make sure you include the data sources you will use, the appropriate collection methods, and who will be responsible for collecting the data. If you are going to use random sampling, make sure that you have large enough groups to get statistically significant data for analysis.

---

[7] These suggestions draw heavily from "Top Ten Tips for Writing Effective Evaluations" by Rebecca Shawver from *Grants and Foundation Review*, April 19, 2006. http://charitychannel.com/enewsletters/gfr/

4. Name the staff person(s) who will be responsible for data collection and describe their qualifications or planned training. If front-line or direct service staff will be collecting data, determine which supervisors will oversee data collection.

5. Have your program staff and managers meet regularly to monitor progress toward goals or benchmarks. Don't wait until the last minute to ask staff for input; they need to be thinking about the program's progress on an ongoing basis.

6. Schedule quarterly reviews of goal attainment and meeting timelines. Use them to collect information for management and to keep your funders up to date on program performance. Report the results back to program staff and, if appropriate, to clients or participants; don't leave them disconnected from how their program is performing.

7. As part of your qualitative evaluation, plan satisfaction surveys using both structured and open-ended instruments. Of course, ask program participants about the program's impact on their lives and its relevance, as well as about their interactions with staff. In addition, ask your community partners about their views of the program's performance, its community impact, and the quality of your collaborative relationships.

8. Indicate how evaluation results will be used. If you will use data to make program modifications, tell how you will do this and on what schedule. Name the manager or position title authorized to approve program modifications. Say that funders will be notified of any significant program changes prior to implementation.

Research-Based Concepts in Evaluation | 11

Evidence-Based Practices

Nonprofits and grantwriters are increasingly being asked to use evidence-based practices (EBPs) in applying for government funding, and this is causing major shifts in funding and accountability. Evidence-based practices are the other side of evaluation—they're programs that have had a rigorous randomized study (evaluation) with statistically significant results.

Funders like EBPs because they increase the chances that the programs they pay for will get positive results. They also provide a bit of political cover from charges that they're wasting money on unproven programs, so EBP (or related language) gets written into legislation with little understanding of what it means or of the repercussions. The No Child Left Behind Act was a prime example, requiring use of "science-based" programs with the result that many states are pushing their K–12 curricula toward test preparation and finding that there aren't enough psychometricians (the specialists who design "valid and reliable" tests) to produce the tests.

As a grantwriter or nonprofit professional, you may come across RFP requirements to use EBPs in the program you're proposing. When you do, you need to be clear what the funder is asking for, first by talking to their program staff, if possible, but also by looking at the agency's Web page or one of the sites listed later in this chapter. The agency may suggest a list of approved program models or even require a particular model. The program directors in your organization may be familiar with the literature in the field and with programs that have been designed for replication. This can be fairly technical, so you need to be sure you and they understand what's being asked for before writing your proposal.

Evidence-based practices can work to your advantage even when they aren't required. If you're introducing a new program in your community based on a model that has been used successfully elsewhere, showing the model's evidence basis can help with foundation funding. If on the other hand your organization has developed a strong program model, a good evaluation can put it on the track to becoming an evidence-based practice, which can help you with future funding and possibly lead to your program being replicated elsewhere. It helps to become evidence-based if your evaluation results are published in a peer-reviewed academic journal, if your evaluator is a PhD, and if one of your agency's senior management staff is listed as a co-author of the article.

Evidence-based has several slightly differing definitions, and terms like evidence-based, research-based, blueprint program, model program, proven practice, promising practice, best practice, and effective are sometimes used interchangeably. However, many agencies have a hierarchy of practices, with evidence-based being the top rated, proven next, and promising lower. Figure 11-1 gives a good rough idea of what you can use in deciding where a practice or program falls on the spectrum.

Figure 11-1. Levels of Evidence-Based Practice

Evidence-Based Practice	Proven Practice	Promising Practice
• Randomized comparison group	• Nonrandomized comparison group or quasi-experimental study	• No comparison group or not randomized
• Consistent evidence of success (at least two studies)	• One successful study	• No studies or informal studies
• Statistically significant improvement compared to an alternative practice or no intervention	• Statistically significant improvement compared to an alternative practice or no intervention	• May have evidence of success, often based on consensus opinions of providers, but not scientifically proven
• Can be replicated	• Can be replicated	

In many cases, funders or reviewers may require higher standards of proof or of replicability, such as:

- Must be published in peer-reviewed journals.

- More studies with the same results required (at least three).

- Positive outcomes in both scientifically controlled and routine care settings.

- Sample sizes for both treatment and comparison group of more than a specified amount (usually greater than 30).

- "Meaningful outcomes" that help clients achieve important goals or objectives.

- "Substantial" effect, defined as outcomes changed at least 20% and statistically significant at the 5% level.

- A "fidelity scale" tool that can be used to ensure that a replicated program is being implemented in a manner consistent with the original evidence-based treatment model.

Problems with Evidence-Based Practices

Although EBPs have much utility and can help organizations to provide better services to their clients, they can also have a dark side. As mentioned with the No Child Left Behind Act, they can distort an entire field by poorly thought-out requirements. Here are some other problems with them:

- The EBP paradigm is based on hard science and is heavily weighted toward quantitative research, using randomized control groups and looking for statistical validity. However, it is weak on the qualitative side and rarely shows how, why, and for whom the program is effective.

- Local service organizations, which have developed effective programs in their own communities, rarely have had the money or expertise to have their programs scientifically studied. In many cases the program isn't large enough to provide both treatment and control groups. They may be pressured to abandon the successful program they have developed and adopt a national model that may be expensive, complex, and require extensive modification to fit local conditions.

- Minority organizations working with particular ethnic groups may find EBPs aren't culturally appropriate for their community or target population. Since most EBPs are based on studies of particular populations, they often reflect the needs of that group. For example, two Native American service organizations I have worked with are struggling to get their programs defined as evidence-based so they can continue receiving state funding, even though they are widely acknowledged to be excellent and effective programs.

- Some EBPs have demonstrated positive outcomes in an artificially controlled study (what scientists call *efficacy*), but not in the real-world conditions most nonprofits work in (what scientists call *effectiveness*).

You may encounter two other issues when implementing evidence-based programs. An original program was based on particular methods, protocols, and practices. To assume that your program will have the same results, your staff must have the same training, follow the same policies and procedures, and utilize the same methods as the original. And to ensure this, two vehicles have been developed.

- A **fidelity scale tool** may be required to ensure that you are following the original model—in effect, an ongoing formative evaluation to guarantee compliance.

- The program may have manuals for the staff to follow in program delivery. This is called a **manualized program**.

The Changing Landscape of Evidence-Based Practices

In my backyard of Portland, Oregon, many changes have been introduced in the last few years. The same things are happening across America at the local, state, and federal level, as well as within private agencies. The impact on nonprofits, local government, and grantwriting is immense.

United Way of the Columbia–Willamette. The following is an excerpt from a story about United Way that appeared in *The Oregonian* on June 2, 2006.

> United Way giveth and—well, it doesn't taketh away, but it inevitably disappoints many with its funding allocation for 2006. More than 100 social service agencies requested a total of $15,895,133 from United Way of the Columbia–Willamette, which has only $4,456,616 to give. That sum will be distributed among 50 to 113 agencies that requested money. Those receiving funds and those not were notified this week.
>
> The money is being awarded according to a new model that emphasizes observable results on the local level, according to United Way officials. "We call it a transition from core funding to community impact funding, and it began five years ago," said Howard Klink, vice president for community impact. "The emphasis is on providing the most practical help to citizens in greatest need." . . .
>
> Funding proposals were required to be as specific as possible about who would be helped, what their needs are, how much money they need, how it would be spent and how they would measure results . . . Wherever possible, Klink said, "We want to produce measurable results. We want people to see that we offer real help."

The shift to the delivery of services based on scientific evidence of effectiveness is a major conceptual change. For example, in both the mental health and addiction treatment systems, this shift includes a focus on lifelong recovery for people with mental illness and substance abuse disorders.

The 2003 Oregon Legislature passed a law that requires increasing amounts of state funds be focused on evidence-based practices for certain agencies that deal with corrections or human services. State agencies are using this "opportunity" to work with stakeholders to restructure their delivery systems for adults and youth. For 2005–2007, the statute requires that at least 25 percent of state funds be used for the provision of evidence-based practices. In 2007–2009, the percentage of funds to be spent on EBPs increases to 50 percent, and in 2009–2011 to 75 percent.

As a result of the legislative mandate, not only state agencies but local government grant programs that use state funds must include EBP requirements in their RFPs. These have resulted in major changes for programs that had been state funded and previously were judged on agency history and capacity to deliver services, rather than program design and effectiveness.

City of Portland Children's Investment Fund. In 2002, the City of Portland's voters approved a ballot measure that created the Children's Investment Fund, providing approximately $8.5 million a year for five years to support programs designed to help children arrive at school ready to learn, provide safe and constructive after-school alternatives for kids, and prevent child abuse and neglect and family violence.

The ballot language said that eligible programs must demonstrate they are cost effective and have a proven record of success. The city interpreted this to include evidence-based practices, among other success measures.

Best Practices

Although the terms *evidence-based practices* and *best practices* are sometimes used interchangeably, in fact they have different roots and meanings. EBPs grew out of scientific research, and best practices come from business management and are more likely to be based on practitioners' experience than on theory. The term *best practice* generally refers to the best possible way of doing something, in the opinion of people in the field. It is commonly used in business, software engineering, medicine, and increasingly by governments and international organizations. Something can be a best practice without having been studied, if it is agreed upon in the field that it works well *in practice*. Generally the term connotes an innovative approach that can be used as a model by others in the same field.

Benchmarks and Baselines

Two other research-based concepts that you are likely to run across in your grantwriting are benchmarks and baselines.

Benchmarks[8] are performance data used for comparative purposes, generally for setting organizational goals. They may be internal—looking at your own organization's historical performance—or external—looking at the performance of leaders in your field, and using their results as a target. Benchmarks are generally used to set goals for entire organizations rather than for individual programs. The federal government and several states have set benchmarks for particular areas such as education or for the whole of state government. You may encounter benchmarks in government, community foundation, or United Way RFPs. Referring to state benchmarks in grant proposals is a way of tying your program to the larger community and demonstrating your knowledge of the broader picture.

For example, Healthy People 2010 is the U.S. government's benchmarks for the American people's health. It used leading health indicators[9] that were important public health issues, that had available data for measuring progress, and that could motivate individuals and communities to action. Many healthcare-related federal grant RFPs ask how your program relates to Healthy People 2010.

Baselines are the facts about your community or your clients before your grant program begins; you will measure your program's progress against these to determine your program's impact. Baselines can come from your agency records tracking client performance, from census or local government data describing your target population, or from the pre-program test of your program participants. This is all information you may put in a grant proposal's needs statement, but it should also be used for setting your goals and objectives.

Baseline data is something you should have begun collecting yesterday. This is an area where the grantwriter needs to work with program staff. Talk to the program managers and see what information the staff is collecting, and whether it is more than just outputs (numbers of counseling sessions, etc.). If they aren't tracking client outcomes, encourage them to set up systems for doing so. Numbers are simply digits on paper until the reader can draw meaningful conclusions from them.

---

[8] The Wilder Foundation has an excellent book titled *Benchmarking for Nonprofits*. It's listed in the bibliography.

[9] The leading health indicators are physical activity, overweight/obesity, tobacco use, substance abuse, responsible sexual behavior, mental health, violence and injury, environmental quality, immunization, and access to health care.

Someone else's baseline data, or the lack of it, can also be a problem. Once I was working on a Byrne[10] grant for a youth gang program, and at the bidder's conference, the state program officer said they wanted our programs to demonstrate a 20 percent reduction in recidivism in our proposals. I raised my hand and asked, "Do you have current recidivism figures?" He said no. "Does anybody?" No again. "Well," I asked, "How are we supposed to measure the reduction, then?" We managed to get the requirement modified.

This was the not uncommon occurrence of a poorly thought out RFP. However, even if they had had the numbers, it would have been difficult for us to track and measure for several reasons.

- Once youth left our program, we had no way of knowing if they had reoffended.

- In Oregon, as in many states, when a youth turns 18, they leave the juvenile justice system and enter the adult system. The agencies are different, and their records are entirely separate. There's no way, without serious time and expense, to track someone from one system to the other.

- How did they want to define recidivism? Say we had a kid who was adjudicated for attempted murder and assault (we had several). Of course, if he got a gun and shot at someone, that's recidivism. If he was picked up for jaywalking, did that count as an offense? How about violating curfew? Shoplifting? Possession of alcohol? A lot of the definition depended on his relationship with his probation officer, which was out of our control.

---

[10] The Edward Byrne Memorial State and Local Law Enforcement Assistance Grant Program is a U.S. Department of Justice state pass-through program.

Using an Outside Evaluator | 12

IN MANY CASES, with larger grants and complex projects, you'll want or need to hire an outside evaluator. Sometimes you'll want to prove the effectiveness of a program and need someone with specialized skills to oversee control groups, do statistical analysis, and so forth.

Why Use an Outside Evaluator?

Of the many reasons your organization might want to use an outside evaluator, these are the ones I have found most important.

- **The funder requires it.** Many federal grants require you to budget 10 or 15 percent on evaluation, and may require an outside evaluator. Some larger foundations will also require independent evaluation.

- **You don't have evaluation capacity in-house.** If you're planning a quantitative evaluation with an experimental design and control groups, very likely you won't have the expertise in your organization to do the instrument design, select control groups, and handle statistical analysis.

- **An outsider brings credibility.** You may want to use an independent and credentialed outsider because your program is controversial, highly visible, rapidly changing, or because you need to establish (or restore) credibility to your program or organization. An evaluator's credibility may come because of their independence or their expertise. In most cases you'll be looking for both.

- **An outsider may be able to get information that your program can't.** If your organization provides mandated services and participants could fear losing services or being punished, they may not give their true opinions to your staff. An outside person who is able to prove their independence may gain access or get truer responses than your staff. (Examples could be a probation department or an alcohol and drug treatment program).

Figure 12-1. Pros and Cons of Using Outside Evaluators

Pros	Cons
• Less work for your organization • Professional expertise • Objectivity • Results may have more credibility	• Less control over the process • Staff may have more complete understanding of your program • Less opportunity to develop internal evaluation capacity • Expense

Finding an Outside Evaluator

If you plan to use an outside evaluator, choose one early. Don't succumb to the temptation to make the evaluator a "to be determined" person, if that can be avoided. Having the evaluator identified and involved will demonstrate your professionalism.

In addition to being able to use their credentials in your proposal, try to involve them in planning your grant proposal. You want to make sure that your program design is structured so that the evaluation can be statistically valid. Sometimes a professional evaluator will write the evaluation section of your proposal on the understanding that you'll hire them if the grant is funded. If you can't involve the evaluator in grant planning, get them on board as soon as possible after you're funded.

Here are several sources for evaluators:

- **Find an academic:** Evaluators can often be found in local universities and medical schools (or hospitals for health care grants). Formal evaluation is similar to research, and in fact most evaluators' formal training is in research design and statistics. Until a few years ago, it was rare to find classes called "evaluation." When looking for a university evaluator, you can contact the department that works with your field (like social work, sociology, education, or public administration), the Office of Sponsored Research (who oversee faculty research), or see if there's an evaluation office on campus.

- **Consult with a professional:** You'll find professional evaluation firms, as well as individuals, in most cities. Ask other organizations in your community who they have used and liked working with. Check with the American Evaluation Association (www.eval.org) for members in your area.

- **Ask the funder:** Some large foundations and government agencies have lists of evaluators and their areas of expertise. Or you can call agencies who have been funded previously and ask them who they worked with. If a particular name emerges as having worked with the grantees of a particular funding agency, that firm could add credibility to your proposal.

- **Check federal agencies or national trade or advocacy groups:** Many federal agencies have technical assistance Websites with lists of evaluators, such as the What Works Clearinghouse registry of outside evaluators in education (http://www.whatworks.ed.gov/technicalassistance/overview.html).

Choosing an Evaluator

Once you've identified some potential evaluators, you should call a few of them and get general information. Then you might interview those few that seem most promising. Here are a few things to look for:

- **Do they favor a particular type of evaluation?** If an evaluator starts recommending particular evaluation methods before learning what you need to know or how you plan to use the findings, it may indicate a preference for, or experience with, a particular evaluation design. If that's not the kind of evaluation you're looking for, or if you haven't decided, they're probably not a good match for your project.

- **Do they have an agenda?** Check to see if a researcher you're considering brings their own reasons for doing your evaluation. A professor may be writing a book or conducting long-term research; a doctoral student may want to fit your evaluation into a dissertation. Or they may have their own theories that could influence what they expect to find. If their needs mesh with yours, then it's win-win. If they don't, you need to ensure that their work will meet your needs, not just theirs.

- **Can they communicate with your staff and board?** If the evaluator describes the process only in highly technical jargon, that may make it hard for your staff to work with them, whether because of incomprehension or intimidation. It may also be an indication that their reports will be full of jargon and theory, hard to interpret, and hard to use to implement changes.

- **Do they show cultural sensitivity?** If you work in a diverse community, the evaluator needs to be acceptable to the community and able to understand or learn the culture for the evaluation to gather accurate information.

After screening to get a good match, you will probably identify one or two possible evaluators you're most comfortable with. You can then have a more detailed interview, with such questions as:

- How much evaluation have you done, especially in projects similar in size and content to ours?

- Who would be doing our evaluation—a senior staff, junior staff, a grad student? What are their qualifications?

- What are your ownership and confidentiality policies? Do you want or intend to publish an article based on our work? If so, how would our organization be identified? Could one of our senior staff be listed as co-author? Can we approve of our representation in the copy?

- Please provide us with some names of past clients we can talk to.

And be sure to check references!

Once you've decided on an evaluator, you need to write a contract, which should include the following:[11]

- **Scope of work:** This includes defining the organization's information needs and the purpose of the evaluation, defining the Program Theory Model, and identifying constraints (time, money, data availability, politics) and how they will be addressed.

- **Evaluation tasks:** Who does data entry, transcribes interviews, correlates interview answers, writes up reports, and similar tasks?

- **Ownership of the data:** If articles are published, does it need both parties' approval, and who are listed as authors?

- **Fees:** For a full, formal evaluation in a federal grant, 10–15 percent of the total is reasonable. For a smaller proposal to a private foundation, 5 percent may be more likely. To lower costs, the scope of work can be reduced, or some work can be done by the organization.

---

[11] The Evaluation Center at Western Michigan University has a more detailed checklist of things that should be in an evaluation contract, as well as other checklists. http://www.wmich.edu/evalctr/checklists/

- **Timeline:** This should include major steps in the evaluation process, data collection schedules, reports, or other work components and billing deadlines.

- **Contents of reports:** Narrative, charts, literature review, comparison to national or other statistics, number of drafts and who edits them.

- **Division of responsibilities:** Figure 12-2 below shows some typical responsibilities.

Figure 12-2. Evaluator and Organization Responsibilities

Evaluator Responsibilities	Organization Responsibilities
• Develop an evaluation plan, in conjunction with staff • Train project staff • Design or select data collection instruments • Implement data collection procedures • Establish and oversee confidentiality procedures • Write progress and final evaluation reports • Attend staff, board, and funder meetings • Present findings to board and possibly conferences	• Educate the evaluator about the program or project • Provide feedback about data collection tools for appropriateness and relevance • Keep evaluator informed of program changes • Specify information to be included in report • Assist in interpreting evaluation findings • Monitor contract and timeline • Supervise in-house activities such as data collection and data entry • Keep communications open among staff, clients, and evaluator

Working with an Evaluator

The Association of Baltimore Area Grantmakers' Website has this list of tips for managing your evaluation. Look under publications for "When and how to use External Evaluators" at www.abagmd.org.

- **Establish a desired communication pattern** early and in writing. One person should be the point of contact for the consulting team— that person should facilitate contact with others, provide advice and guidance to the team, and gather additional information and/or resources to support the evaluation when necessary.

- **Maintain communication** throughout the project. You'll need to know how the work is coming along, and the consultant needs to be informed about things that arise at the foundation.

- **Develop strategies** for monitoring the *work* of the consultants (not just deliverables). You may want to accompany the evaluation team on some site visits. Are they organized? Do they work well with grantees? Are they doing everything that they said they would do and in a manner with which you are comfortable?

- **Seek input** from grantees or other sources. Were they comfortable with the evaluator's approach?

- **Don't be a terrible client!** Remember that consultants get paid for their *time*—every call, meeting, and presentation "uses up" valuable contract time. Do what you can to facilitate their work—don't make it harder on them. If you want or need much more than was anticipated, expect to PAY more for it!

| 13

NOW LET'S SEE what some grant proposal evaluation sections might look like. I created some model nonprofit organizations to use as examples in *Understanding Nonprofit Finances* and am using them again here, along with some new ones.

- **Fairview Terrace:** An assisted living facility for very low income seniors.

- **Florentine Chamber Orchestra (FCO):** A high-quality, mid-sized performing arts organization.

- **Jefferson County Community Action (JCCA):** A well-established social service organization that runs several programs.

Below are five examples that are designed to give you the feel of different approaches for programs and funders of different sizes. They all follow the same format: The type of grant and funder are in bold type, followed by a brief description of the project. Next are the funder's evaluation requirements. Then the proposal evaluation section is presented inside a box.

1. **Fairview Terrace: From a Small Grant Proposal by Letter to a Family Foundation.** This project is for the Fairview Terrace staff to use volunteers to educate family members of elderly residents of long-term care facilities about their loved ones' mental health, changes in health, accessing Medicare, and other issues of aging.

Evaluation requirement: Present plans for evaluating the effectiveness of the project.

This model will be evaluated with three different populations of elders, providing feedback useful to social service professionals throughout the state. The project will be evaluated by the Markham University School of Social Work and the chief executive of Fairview Terrace.

The evaluation will include:

- Seeing whether the planned numbers of volunteers were trained and utilized

- Reviewing curriculum, manuals, and materials developed by the project

- Conducting customer satisfaction surveys with residents and families, using a 5-point Likert scale and data from a comparison group

- Conducting interviews with volunteers and staff about program quality, outcomes, and effectiveness.

2. **Florentine Chamber Orchestra: From a Proposal to a General Purpose Foundation.** This project is for marketing and audience development.

Evaluation requirement: Present methods and criteria for assessing the project's effectiveness.

The project will be evaluated on an ongoing basis by the Florentine Chamber Orchestra (FCO) Board based on three main criteria:

- **Performance:** Are high-quality materials being produced and distributed as shown in this grant proposal? Are the listed goals being met? Is the timetable being followed? Are grant funds being spent and accounted for as budgeted?

- **Results:** Are audiences increasing at FCO concerts? Are season ticket sales, contributions, and underwriting increasing to meet projections? Is public awareness of FCO increasing, as shown by telephone inquiries, newspaper coupons received, and individual concert ticket sales?

- **Purpose:** Is FCO becoming financially self-sufficient as a result of this project? Are season ticket holders renewing? Is FCO becoming known in Madison County and elsewhere as a high-quality, professional orchestra? Is FCO attracting and holding top-quality musicians as a result of increased audiences and revenues?

   3. **Fairview Terrace: From a Capital Proposal to a General Purpose Foundation.** This grant is part of Fairview Terrace's capital campaign to build an assisted living facility for very low-income residents of an inner city neighborhood.

   Evaluation requirement: Present methods and criteria for assessing the project's effectiveness.

The Fairview Terrace Board of Directors and Advisory Council will assess this project using the following three major criteria:

- **Construction:** Was the facility's construction satisfactorily completed? Was the timetable followed and deadlines met? Was the construction within the overall project budget? Were grant funds spent and accounted for as budgeted? Does the building design meet the needs of residents and staff? This evaluation will be made after construction is completed in the Spring of 2008.

- **Operations:** Is the Fairview Terrace Assisted Living Facility (ALF) operating at full occupancy? Is it self-supporting with Medicaid funding? Is it meeting all state and local licensing requirements? Is it meeting the financial and operating goals set by the board? Are all parts of ALF operations (food, medical care, social life, counseling, etc.) being managed well? Are strong relationships being maintained among Fairview Terrace, nursing schools, and other agencies?

- **Purpose:** Is the Fairview Terrace ALF allowing very low-income Jefferson County residents to live longer, happier, healthier lives while aging in place? Does the Assisted Living Facility support Fairview Terrace values of individuality, independence, dignity, autonomy, and privacy? Are Fairview Terrace ALF residents pleased with the building and the program? Is the Assisted Living Facility presenting new client service options to Fairview Terrace outreach programs and other social service and housing agencies?

---

   4. **Jefferson County Community Action: From a Grant Proposal to a State Department of Education for the 21st Century Community Learning Center.** The 21st Century Community Learning Center (21CCLC) grant is a federal pass-through program. The project is an extensive after-school education program run in school buildings by Jefferson County Community Action (JCCA).

   Evaluation requirements: Describe your plan for acquiring, conducting, and reporting all evaluation data to the State Department of Education (SDOE). Describe how evaluation data will be used to refine, improve, and strengthen the program.

The JCCA will ensure that the following procedures will be used in the evaluation process:

- **Who will collect the data:** Data will be collected initially by JCCA after-school program site managers and school district. JCCA will lend the support of an evaluation research liaison to the site efforts to administer evaluation tools and enter data in the JCCA Database. The evaluation research liaison and JCCA staff will ensure the high quality of data collected and will centralize data for analysis. JCCA will also provide technical assistance on the JCCA Database to the sites, including training and troubleshooting; creation of new reports and queries; and addition of new capabilities as needed.

- **When data will be collected:** Ongoing data collection by JCCA site managers using the JCCA Database, and by the school district, on student grades, attendance, and behavior. Initial assessment (and pre-program testing) of students' reading and math skill levels using Measures of Academic Progress (MAP) will be conducted at the beginning and end of the school year by the school district and shared with JCCA. JCCA may choose also to conduct mid-year MAP assessment to check progress and make any program changes. Behavioral data will be collected at the beginning and end of JCCA prevention and early intervention programs. Although not explicitly listed in the 21CCLC performance measures, this pre- and post-program testing will also measure increase in skills in adults and children, decrease in social isolation of parents, and increase in school participation by parents.

- **What data collection methods will be used:** JCCA Database (registration and tracking system), pre- and post-program testing, skill assessment tests, school district data collection system.

- **How data will be analyzed:** JCCA will draw on the existing cadre of evaluators involved an overall JCCA program evaluation to analyze the data from the various sources. JCCA currently contracts with Jefferson University to analyze student achievement data.

- **How reports will be disseminated to SDOE and the public:** JCCA will compile and format reports and ensure their timely dissemination to SDOE and the public. Dissemination to SDOE will happen through the reporting mechanisms required by 21CCLC at state and federal levels. The JCCA staff is familiar with the 21CCLC format. Any additional evaluation reports will be provided to SDOE upon completion. Dissemination of reports to the public will happen through the strong existing communications structures that JCCA has in place.

- **How evaluation data will be used to improve programs:** Embedded in the JCCA after-school program, and demonstrated in our process evaluation, is a structure for continuous quality improvement. Analysis of evaluation data and reports will be disseminated among and reviewed by JCCA staff, JCCA site managers, and partners. JCCA program development specialists and evaluators will lead planning sessions with JCCA site managers to translate data findings into changes that will improve and strengthen the program. Data will also be available on an on-going basis to individual school staff through the JCCA Database, which is a daily management and tracking tool. This more regular data will be used to make any program refinements necessary to achieve the identified goals.

5. **Jefferson County Community Action: From a Demonstration Grant to the Centers for Disease Control and Prevention for School-Based Violence Prevention.** Jefferson County Community Action operates programs in both the community and the schools. This example is a full-scale, quantitative, experimental design evaluation for a federal grant.

Evaluation requirements: Program monitoring: The extent to which the design to monitor program implementation (including a data analysis plan) is clearly described and is appropriate for the target group, program, data collection opportunities, and proposed project period. The extent to which data collection, data processing, and management activities are clearly described. The extent to which the proposed goals and objectives are clearly stated, time-phased, and measurable.

Design of Program Monitoring

Evaluator

The evaluation will be conducted by ABC Research Corporation under the direction of Sally Jones, MSW, JD. ABC and Jefferson County Community Action (JCCA) have maintained a five-year research–practitioner relationship through previously funded CDC and Oregon Department of Justice work in the area of youth violence prevention (VP). The current proposal will expand and extend JCCA's successful work with older children to their younger counterparts in the elementary schools and community in which JCCA has worked since 1981.

Measures

The evaluation will employ both process and outcome measures using a variety of data collection approaches: interviews with staff and students, structured observations of program and students, self-report surveys of students (grades 4 and 5) and their parents, and assembly of extant data from school and district records.

Process data will be collected from JCCA staff and structured observations of JCCA violence prevention program activities. Quarterly observations of program activities will be conducted by ABC Research staff at each grade and school on a rotating basis. These observations will focus on the violence prevention curriculum (conflict resolution, anger management, mediation) and the JCCA curriculum (academic support, social behavior guidance, and reinforcement of the JCCA Standards). They will assess the fidelity of implementation of these activities and rate the level of participation of the students and the interactions between JCCA staff and students. These data will be summarized and shared with JCCA administrative and school-based staff at monthly meetings. Interpretations from the JCCA staff and discussion with ABC Research staff will generate ideas for any needed adjustments in program implementation and begin to build a compendium of information of potential value to others who are interested in replicating the JCCA program. Individual, school-based JCCA staff will also be interviewed by ABC Research staff to obtain their perceptions of program implementation and its influence on the students.

In addition, JCCA staff will maintain logs of their individual contacts with students. These logs will both quantify the amount of time spent with students and categorize the nature of these contacts along a number of dimensions previously found as descriptive of these interactions. A sample contact log form, used in other violence prevention evaluation activities with JCCA, is included in the Appendix to this proposal.

Outcome data will be collected from students, parents, and staff. A random sample of students ($n = 5$) from each grade and school in the JCCA-VP and Control groups (total $n = 120$) will be interviewed each year to assess their exposure to violence, tendencies toward aggressive behavior, relationships with other students, skills in peacefully negotiating potentially violent situations, attitudes and commitment to school, and their own cultural or ethnic identity. Half of these students will be randomly assigned to be interviewed in the fall, and the other half in the spring. The interview protocol will be adapted from a twenty-item instrument used in the Peace Builders program (Embry et al., 1996) and a ten-item scale used in the Super Stars program (Emshoff et al., 1996). Both programs were implemented at the elementary school level with a majority of African American and Hispanic students among their participants. The interviews will also contain brief measures of the children's exposure to violence (Richters and Martinez, 1990) and their skills in resolving potentially violent interpersonal scenarios peacefully (Aber et al., 1995).

Brief paper and pencil self-report surveys will be administered to all students at the 4th and 5th grade levels in all three study groups in the fall and spring of each year. Both Peace Builders and Super Stars programs have used this approach, carefully adapting standardized scales to adjust for the reading levels and attention spans of this age group. Standardized scales adapted for this use will include the Conflict Behavior Questionnaire (Robin and Foster, 1989), the delinquency and aggressive behavior scales of the Youth Self-Report (Achenbach, 1991), peer influences on delinquent behavior developed by Patterson and Dishion (1985), the School and Family Bonding scales from the Individual Protective Factors Index (Phillips and Springer, 1992), and a Values scale developed for this age group by Belgrave et al. (1997). The full instrument will be constructed such that it can be administered during a single class period in the school or JCCA Center. Its length will be well under the 100-item self-report scales used successfully by Peace Builders.

Structured observations of students during recess will be conducted on randomly selected days, once per month per school, across the school year. Two ABC Research staff will conduct these observations using the structured protocol developed by Peace Builders. Aggressive behavior, peer interactions, and supervisor and staff interactions with students will be coded during prescribed time intervals. JCCA staff will assist in the coding of data by differentiating between JCCA-VP students and Control students in the observations. These observations will also be conducted in the JCCA Center each month. Summaries of these observations will also be shared with JCCA staff during the monthly meetings described earlier.

Parents of all students involved in the study will be surveyed annually by mail ($n = 400$). Telephone follow-ups will be conducted among nonrespondents. In addition to basic demographic items, the surveys will include the Moos & Moos (1986) Family Conflict and Family Environment scales, the Achenbach (1991) Child Behavior Checklist aggressive and delinquent behavior subscales (adult counterparts to the Youth Self Report subscales administered to the students), and an adaptation of the Phinney (1992) Ethnic Identity scale to determine the extent to which their African American culture and roots are important aspects of the home environment.

Finally, extant data on the school attendance, grade point average, progress on school district and Oregon state mastery criteria, and violence-related disciplinary referrals will be assembled on an annual basis for all participating students.

Data Collection and Analysis

As stated earlier, the proposed program will be conducted in the three elementary schools served by JCCA and will involve children in grades 2 through 5. Three groups of students will be included in the study: a JCCA treatment group (JCCA-VP, $n = 150$), who will participate in the proposed program; a JCCA Center comparison group, consisting of students referred to JCCA (but not enrolled in the full JCCA program, which will include the proposed violence prevention program) from the same schools and grades, who will receive some support services at the recently completed JCCA Center for Self Enhancement (JCCA Center, estimated $n = 100^*$) ; and a no-treatment control group selected from the same grades and schools who will receive no violence prevention program or JCCA services (Control, $n = 250$).

The inclusion of the JCCA Center group allows the evaluation the opportunity to test the added value of the proposed violence prevention program (i.e., JCCA-VP) to other support services provided by JCCA (i.e., the Center program). The Control group will be assembled using the method employed by Gabriel et al. (1996) in the previous middle and high school violence prevention evaluation. Eleven matching criteria (e.g., demographic, school performance, home and neighborhood environment) were used in selecting a similar group of students. Analysis of the target behaviors at baseline indicated substantial equivalence of the JCCA program and matched control groups. A copy of the control group selection form and criteria is included in the Appendix to this proposal.

The quasi-experimental, cross-sectional design for the evaluation study is depicted in Figure A.

Figure A. Evaluation Design

Grade	Group	Year 1	Year 2	Year 3	Year 4
Grade 2	JCCA-VP				
	JCCA Center				
	Control				
Grade 3	JCCA-VP				
	JCCA Center				
	Control				
Grade 4	JCCA-VP				
	JCCA Center				
	Control				
Grade 5	JCCA-VP				
	JCCA Center				
	Control				

* Students referred to JCCA by teachers, school administrators, or parents who cannot be served due to caseload limitations are eligible to participate in activities at Jefferson County Community Action at a nominal cost.

This participation is entirely voluntary and self-selecting and, at this point, a precise number is not known. Recent history suggests that an enrollment of 100 students from these schools and grades is a reasonable, and perhaps conservative, estimate. These students represent a demographically similar, and highly accessible for data collection, group to use for comparative purposes in the evaluation.

As depicted in the design, the program will serve students in grades 2–5 in each of the four years of the proposed study: 150 JCCA-VP students, 100 JCCA Center students (estimated), and 150 matched Control students. The design is cross-sectional rather than longitudinal, with fifth grade students "graduating out" of the elementary program and a new group of second graders added each year. Some longitudinal comparisons will be available, however. The shaded area of the design figure depicts the largest of these—students who begin the program at second grade and continue through the four years of the proposed intervention.

Data Collection and Management

The schedule for data collection, using all of the measures and methods described above, is shown in Figure B. This schedule will be repeated for each year of the proposed project.

Figure B. Proposed Data Collection Schedule

Quarter	Q1			Q2			Q3			Q4		
Month	O	N	D	J	F	M	A	M	J	J	A	S
Process Data:												
Program observations	X	X	X	X	X	X	X	X				X
Staff interviews		X			X			X			X	
Staff discussions	X	X	X	X	X	X	X	X	X	X	X	X
Contact logs	X	X	X	X	X	X	X	X	X	X	X	X
Outcome Data:												
Student interviews	X	X					X	X				
Student surveys	X							X				
Playground observations	X	X	X	X	X	X	X	X				X
Parent surveys								X				
Extant data (school)										X	X	

All data collected will be entered on a relational PC database developed by ABC Research staff during previous CDC-funded violence prevention evaluation activities. The database consists of relational files with student demographic, parent, and other friends and family location information, and evaluation data collected in previous studies. The locator information is particularly critical in longitudinal studies as a safeguard against attrition.

Currently, the database includes information on over 700 students in grades 2–12 who participate in any of JCCA's program activities (including Control group students for evaluation purposes). Only minor additions to this data management tool will be needed to ensure its usefulness for the currently proposed project.

Data Analysis and Statistical Power

Qualitative data collected in the process evaluation will be analyzed using methods described by Miles and Huberman (1994). Responses to open-ended questions and qualitative observations will be coded and synthesized to document common themes and patterns across the data. Where possible, these codes will be transformed to quantitative indicators to include in the analysis described below (e.g., the perceptions of staff as to fidelity of implementation of the program). Much of the qualitative data will, however, be analyzed via the inductive process needed to ascertain the common themes in the data that will assist in the interpretation of quantitative data.

The data analytic strategy for the quantitative data collected will include descriptive, correlational, and inferential analysis methods. Within each of these methods, the particular statistical technique will be determined based on the scaling properties of the data. Where dichotomous prevalence rates are involved (e.g., the number of students engaging in aggressive behavior during playground observations, or the number of students endorsing a particular conflict resolution strategy during the interviews), techniques will include proportions, chi-square tests of homogeneity and independence, and logistic regression for descriptive, correlational, and inferential methods, respectively. Where data are continuous (e.g., students' scores on the School Bonding scale or parents' scores on the Family Conflict scale), techniques will include means and standard deviations, Pearson correlations, and analysis of variance and covariance (ANOVA and ANCOVA).

Logistic regression will be used to compare the prevalence rates of students in the three study groups on outcomes such as their incidence of aggressive behavior or disciplinary referrals during each year of the project, adjusting for baseline rates of these behaviors and background characteristics such as age (grade) and gender. An illustrative model for the analysis is as follows:

$$Y = a + b_1X_1 + b_2X_2 + b_3X_3 + b_4X_4 + b_5X_5$$

Where:

Y = the outcome in the current year

X_1 = the baseline value of the outcome

X_2 = age (grade) of the student

X_3 = gender of the student

X_4, X_5 = dummy variables for group

Multivariate analysis of variance and covariance will be used to test the design effects shown in Figure A (group by grade level) on continuous outcome measures in a given year. Repeated measures ANOVA will be used to assess the trends over time on these outcomes for those longitudinal cohorts described earlier in this section of the proposal.

Finally, the statistical power of the analyses proposed for the study is shown by illustration (selecting one particular analytical method and group comparison). The calculations, using the conventional "small," "medium," and "large" effect sizes of Cohen (1988) assume a Type I error rate of .05 and nondirectional (i.e., two-tailed) hypothesis test. Testing for group differences at a single point in time with the proposed sample sizes yields statistical power estimates of .99 for both medium (.25 SD) and large (.40 SD) effect sizes, but a far more modest power of .24 for small effect sizes. Thus, if the JCCA program produces moderate to large effects, the proposed design and analysis has a very high probability of detecting them. If, however, the effects are small and more subtle, there is only about a one-in-four chance of detecting them as statistically significant.

References

Aber, J. L.; Brown, J. L.; Jones, S.; & Samples, F. (1995). *Adapting measures of children's beliefs, attributions, and skills for use in the evaluation of violence prevention programs.* New York, NY: National Center for Children in Poverty, Columbia University.

Achenbach, T. M. (1991a). *Manual for the Youth Self Report and 1991 Profile.* Burlington, VT: Univ. of Vermont Dept. of Psychiatry.

Achenbach, T. M. (1991b). *Manual for the Child Behavior Checklist/4-18 and 1991 Profile.* Burlington, VT: Univ. of Vermont Dept. of Psychiatry.

Belgrave, F. Z.; Townsend, T. G; Cherry, V. G.; & Cunningham, D. M. (1997). The influence of an Afrocentric worldview and demographic variables on drug knowledge, attitudes and use among African American youth. *Journal of Community Psychology, 25*(5), 421–434.

Cohen, J. (1988). *Statistical Power Analysis in the Behavioral Sciences, 2nd Edition.* New York: Academic Press.

Embry, D. D.; Flannery, D. J.; Vazsonyi, A. T.; Powell, K. E.; & Atha, H. (1996). PeaceBuilders: A theoretically driven, school-based model for early violence prevention. *American Journal of Preventive Medicine, 12*(5), 91–100.

Emshoff, J.; Avery, E; Raduka, G.; Anderson, D. J.; & Calvert, C. (1996). Findings from Super Stars: A health promotion program for families to enhance multiple protective factors. *Journal of Adolescent Health, 11*(1), 68–95.

Gabriel, R. M.; Hopson, T. L.; Haskins, M.; & Powell, K. E. (1996). Building relationships and resilience in the prevention of youth violence. *American Journal of Preventive Medicine, 12*(5).

Moos, R. H.; & Moos, B. S. (1986). *Family Environment Scale Manual.* Palo Alto, CA.: Consulting Psychologists.

Patterson, G. R.; & Dishion, T. (1985). Contributions of families and peers to delinquency, *Criminology, 23,* 63–79.

Phillips, J.; & Springer, J. F. (1992). *Extended national youth sports program 1991-92 evaluation highlights, part two: Individual Protective Factors Index and risk assessment study.* Report prepared for the National Collegiate Athletic Association. Sacramento, CA: EMT Associates.

Richters, J. E.; & Martinez, P. *Things I have seen and heard: A structured interview for assessing young children's violence exposure.* Rockville, MD: National Institute of Mental Health.

Robin, A.; & Foster, S. (1989). *Negotiating parent-adolescent conflict.* New York: Guilford.

SECTION THREE

Evaluation Resources

General Information | 14

Internet Resources

1. National Resource Centers Websites

A search of the Web finds dozens of National Resource Centers for numerous issues and program areas. Following are a few of the major ones as examples, but do a search for National Resource Center (your issue) to see if you find information you can use. Some are government sponsored, some are private, and they're of varying quality, but all provide useful information for research.

National Child Welfare Resource Centers. Links to thirteen centers including adoption, child protective services, organizational improvement, legal and judicial issues, child welfare data, family centered practice, and youth development. http://muskie.usm.maine.edu/helpkids/centers.htm

National Resource Center on Domestic Violence. http://www.nrcdv.org/

National Resource and Training Center on Homelessness and Mental Illness. http://www.nrchmi.samhsa.gov/

National Resource Center on Supportive Housing and Home Modification. http://www.usc.edu/dept/gero/nrcshhm/

2. Statistics Websites

The Statistical Abstract of the United States. Published since 1878, this is the authoritative and comprehensive summary of statistics on the social, political, and economic organization of the United States. Sources of data include the Census Bureau, Bureau of Labor Statistics, Bureau of Economic Analysis, and many other federal agencies and private organizations. http://www.census.gov/compendia/statab/

FedStats is devoted to statistical information from over a hundred federal agencies. The statistics can be searched by agency, topic or geographic area. www.fedstats.gov

Kids Count Data Book from the Annie E. Casey Foundation has state by state statistics on children's issues. www.kidscount.org

Economic Statistics Briefing Room provides links to information produced by a number of Federal agencies on employment, income, international, money, output, prices, production, and transportation. http://www .whitehouse.gov/fsbr/esbr.html

Social Statistics Briefing Room provides links to information produced by a number of Federal agencies on crime, demographics, education and health. http://www.whitehouse.gov/fsbr/ssbr.html

The National Center for Education Statistics is the primary federal entity for collecting and analyzing data related to education. http://nces.ed.gov/

Statistics at the State and Local Levels on the FirstGov Website links to statistics and facts on fourteen government Websites. http://www.firstgov .gov/Government/State_Local/Statistics.shtml

General reference government statistics on the FirstGov Website can be found by scrolling down on the left side of the home page to the "Reference Center" and click onto "Data and Statistics." http://www .firstgov.gov/Topics/Reference_Shelf/Data.shtml

University of Michigan Documents Center, "Statistical Resources on the Web" is very helpful and broken down by topic to make it easier to access statistics. www.lib.umich.edu/govdocs/stats.html

Assessing Community Needs—Families and Work Institute (FWI) is a nonprofit center for research that provides data to inform decision-making on the changing workforce, changing family, and changing community. http://www.familiesandwork.org/

3. Publications Websites

Google Scholar provides a simple way to broadly search for scholarly research literature. http://scholar.google.com/

FindArticles.com contains articles from popular magazines and newspapers online, many for free. http://findarticles.com/

The American Institutes for Research (AIR) is a nonprofit behavioral and social science research consulting organization. Their list of publications on various topics is a wonderful place to begin a literature review. http://www.air.org/

Practical Assessment, Research and Evaluation is an online journal of refereed articles on education. http://pareonline.net/

The U.S. Department of Education Publications allows you to search for publications by keyword. http://www.edpubs.org/webstore/content/search.asp

4. Census Websites

A major source of census data is the U.S. Bureau of Census Website. It is also the basic portal to numerous more specific sites, some of which are listed here.

U.S. Bureau of Census allows you to create queries and tables showing percentages that compare national, state, and local statistics. www.census.gov

American Factfinder gives you direct access to the Census Bureau databases and can create a detailed table for any geographic area, from a state down to a census tract. http://factfinder.census.gov/

USA Counties contains almost 6,000 data items for all counties. http://censtats.census.gov/usa/usa.shtml

State and Metropolitan Area Data Book offers comprehensive data for states and metropolitan areas. http://www.census.gov/compendia/smadb/

State & County QuickFacts offers quick, easy access to census facts about people, business, and geography. http://quickfacts.census.gov/qfd/

County & City Databook tracks population and housing data at the local level. http://www.census.gov/statab/www/ccdb.html

CensusScope is an easy-to-use tool for investigating U.S. demographic trends, from the University of Michigan. http://www.ssdan.net/

City-Data.Com has information on American cities, top 100 lists, etc.: www.city-data.com. You can get ZIP-code-level information is available at www.city-data.com/zips/xxxxx.html (insert the actual zip code in place of the x's).

5. Polling Data Websites

Pew Research Center for the People and the Press. http://people-press.org/

The Gallup Organization. http://www.gallup.com/

Harris Interactive provides write-up articles of polling results. http://www.harrisinteractive.com/harris_poll/

The Roper Center is an archive of polls conducted by leading survey research organizations. http://www.ropercenter.uconn.edu/

6. U.S. Government Agency Websites

There are, of course, thousands of government agency Websites. Here are some portals with links to many other sites.

FirstGov is the U.S. Government's Official Web Portal, which gives access to almost all other federal Websites, including agencies. www.firstgov.gov

State and Local Government on the Net is a directory of official state, county, and city government Websites, with links. http://www.statelocalgov.net/

State of the Cities Data Systems is a HUD Website with data for individual metropolitan areas, central cities, and suburbs. http://socds.huduser.org

CDC Wonder provides a single point of access to reports and public health data. http://wonder.cdc.gov

7. Evidence-Based and Best Practices Websites

SAMHSA Model Programs for substance abuse and mental health treatment are "well-implemented, well-evaluated programs" that have been reviewed by SAMHSA's National Registry of Evidence-based Programs and Practices (NREPP). http://modelprograms.samhsa.gov/

Promising Practices Network, operated by the RAND Corporation, is a group of organizations dedicated to providing quality evidence-based information about what works to improve the lives of children, families, and communities. http://www.promisingpractices.net/

Evidence-Based Practice Centers (EPCs) at several institutions in the United States and Canada contract with the Agency for Healthcare Research and Quality to review scientific literature on clinical, behavioral, organizational, and financing topics to produce reports and technology assessments. The EPCs also conduct research on methodology of systematic reviews. http://www.ahrq.gov/clinic/epc/epcenters.htm

The Coalition for Evidence-Based Policy was founded by several major foundations that believe that U.S. social programs are often implemented with little regard to rigorous evidence. Its excellent Website, Social Programs That Work, links to studies in areas such as education, crime and substance abuse, and poverty reduction. In addition to many programs that work, they list the studies that refute such popular programs as DARE and Hawaii Healthy Start. http://www.evidencebasedprograms.org/

The Center for Learning Excellence at Ohio State University maintains a database of evidence-based programs in K–12 education. http://p12.osu .edu/record.php?dataid=48

UN-Habitat Best Practices in Improving the Living Environment is a searchable database that contains over 2,150 proven solutions from more than 140 countries to the common social, economic, and environmental problems of an urbanizing world. http://www.bestpractices.org/

The CDC's Best Practices of Youth Violence Prevention: A Sourcebook for Community Action looks at the effectiveness of specific violence prevention practices in four key areas: parents and families, home visiting, social and conflict resolution skills, and mentoring. Available for download. http://www.cdc.gov/ncipc/dvp/bestpractices.htm

What Works Clearinghouse provides information on replicable educational interventions (programs, products, practices, and policies) to improve student outcomes through a set of easily accessible databases and user-friendly reports. The WWC is administered by the U.S. Department of Education's Institute of Education Sciences. http://www.whatworks.ed.gov/

Center for What Works is a nonprofit working group that assists public and nonprofit organizations to systematically identify and replicate best practices. Links to promising practices, a benchmarking exchange, and similar organizations. http://www.whatworks.org

Childtrends collects and disseminates information about effective programs for children and youth. http://www.childtrends.org/

National Governors Association Center for Best Practices works for the state governors to develop and implement innovative solutions to public policy challenges. Studies and publications on education, healthcare, social and economic issues, technology, and the environment. http://www.nga.org/center/

Libraries

In the last few years we've gotten so used to Googling as our primary source of research that many people have forgotten about the incredible resource available to us all for free—the public library! According to the Institute for Museum and Library Science, America has 122,000 libraries. You can find a list of state libraries at http://lists.webjunction.org/libweb/usa-state.html.

Libraries in a Typical Metropolitan Area (Portland, Oregon)

The following is a list of libraries in the Portland metropolitan area. They are typical of the ones that you may be able to access in your area. For example, the Multnomah County Central Library is located within a few blocks of my office, a dozen other libraries are available to me within walking distance, and even more within just a couple of miles.

Multnomah County Library. The central library and its sixteen branch libraries house a collection of two million book and other materials. It also provides access through interlibrary loan to millions more documents, online full-text magazine and newspaper articles, and databases for research.

Portland State University Library. Although you have to be a student or faculty member to check books out, anyone can use it for research and reading in the building.

Oregon Historical Society (OHS) Research Library. Far more than research for fogies or genealogists, OHS has copies of many publications, old maps, info on ethnic group histories in the City and state, among many other resources.

Portland Art Museum. The museum has its own library of art books.

Multnomah Law Library in the County Courthouse, for any legal research.

Portland Bureau of Planning and Bureau of Development Services Libraries for historical building permits, zoning records (newer ones are on the Web), planning commission records.

Oregon Health & Science University. The state's medical school and major research center libraries are open to the public, and some materials can be checked out for students at area colleges or through the county libraries.

Special and Academic Libraries. There are over 150 special libraries[12] and 27 academic libraries in and around Portland, many of which are open to the public. To find special and academic libraries in your region, check with your state library and ask if they maintain a list.

Bookstores

Retail Bookstores

Bookstores are becoming informal libraries of a sort, with many larger ones (such as Borders or Barnes & Noble) setting up coffee shops or reading areas where you can do research without necessarily buying the books. I'm fortunate to live near Powell's City of Books, the country's largest independent bookstore, which shelves new and used books together.

University Bookstores

When I was first researching for this book, I decided I should take a class in evaluation. I downloaded the Portland State University catalog and did a "find" for "evaluation" and for "research." I found several classes in different departments, but the listings weren't too helpful in deciding which one to take. So I wrote down the course numbers and went to the university bookstore to look for the textbooks, thinking this would help me decide.

What I found was a cornucopia of knowledge presented in various ways by different authors, prescreened and selected for me by the teachers of these classes, authorities on the subject, many with PhDs in their fields. Not only did different departments use different texts, but different professors teaching different sections of the same course used different textbooks. And some of my best finds weren't the required texts, but small paperbacks of supplemental readings.

---

[12] A special library focuses on the interests of the institution it serves, which might be an association, a company, a municipal agency, or other organization. Some are open to the public, some are open restricted hours, and some are closed to the public.

Evaluation Instruments | 15

AS YOU'RE PLANNING your evaluation, you have two choices for choosing evaluation instruments.

- You can design your own, which will be very specific to your project, but this is complex if you're not a trained researcher, as well as time consuming. In addition, you need to put it through an extensive test process to see that it accurately collects the information you need. An exception is basic tally sheets and attendance forms used to track outputs, which can be developed by program staff.

- You can look for existing questionnaires, tests, and interview forms that have been developed and proven by experienced researchers. These have the advantages of having been field-tested, may be known to grant reviewers, and will sometimes come with a data analysis plan.

If you're working with a professional evaluator, they will probably know of some instruments for programs similar to yours. Other local resources include local university faculty and librarians. Talk with other community programs that have conducted similar services, ask if they've done program evaluation and what instruments they used. If you're applying to a government source or a major national foundation, ask them what evaluation tools they recommend. Following are some questions to use in searching for existing instruments.

- Was the instrument designed for programs similar to yours?

- Will the instrument provide data in the form you need?

- Has the instrument been successfully used with a client group similar to yours in terms of race, ethnicity, age, and gender, as well as program issues?

- Does the instrument design fit your program timetable (e.g., does it offer pre- and post-program tests)?

Evaluation-Focused Sites

Tools, Instruments, & Questionnaires for Research & Evaluation of Intervention Programs is produced by the Wilder Foundation. This is a great place to start. It has an index of dozens of instruments, summaries of the instruments (with links for free downloading many of them), information on how to choose an instrument, links to online research tools, and links to major sites on the Web for finding more research instruments. http://www.wilderdom.com/tools.html

American Evaluation Association is devoted to the application and exploration of program and personnel evaluation, technology, and other forms of evaluation. http://www.eval.org/

The Evaluation Exchange is an online magazine from the Harvard Family Research Project, with articles written by the most prominent evaluators in the field. http://gseweb.harvard.edu/~hfrp/eval.html

Community Toolbox, developed by the University of Kansas, is an online guide that addresses practical work on promoting community health and development, with an excellent evaluation section. http://ctb.ku.edu/tools/evaluateinitiative/index.jsp

Innovation Network is a nonprofit organization working to share planning and evaluation tools and know-how. Their Repair Center helps organizations improve, create, and download surveys, interviews, focus groups, questionnaires, and data collection and analysis tools. http://www.innonet.org

Online Evaluation Resource Library (OERL), from SRI International (formerly Stanford Research Institute), was developed by SRI for the National Science Foundation. It includes modules for professionals seeking to design, conduct, document, or review project evaluations as well as examples of evaluation plans, instruments, and reports. http://oerl.sri.com/

The Test Collection of the Educational Testing Service (ETS) has a library of more than 25,000 tests and other measurement devices that makes information on standardized tests and research instruments available to researchers, graduate students, and teachers. Collected from the early 1900s to the present, it is the largest such compilation in the world. To get to the test collection, start at the ETS home page; in the Tests column, select Tests Directory; on the Tests Directory page, scroll down and select Test Link: Home > Tests Directory > Test Link. http://www.ets.org

Online databases such as MedLine, Ebsco, and PsychInfo have pre-established surveys in particular fields. Many university libraries have subscriptions to these services, for example, http://medlineplus.gov/, http://www.apa.org/psycinfo/, http://www.ebsco.com/home/.

Federal Government Evaluation Centers

Several federal agencies have centers for evaluation and research. Their missions and operations differ; some will provide advice in planning evaluation components for their grant programs, others are simply excellent information resources. If you're working on federal grants, check the evaluation center of the agency you're applying to as part of your program planning.

Centers for Disease Control and Prevention (CDC), Evaluation Working Group. http://www.cdc.gov/eval/

National Institutes of Health, Division of Evaluation and Systematic Assessment. http://opasi.nih.gov/desa/eb/

Substance Abuse and Mental Health Services Administration (SAMHSA), Center for Mental Health Services (CMHS), Human Services Research Institute (HSRI), Evaluation Center. http://tecathsri.org/

U.S. Department of Education (DOED), National Center for Research on Evaluation, Standards and Student Testing. http://cresst96.cse.ucla.edu/index.htm

U.S. Department of Education (DOED), Planning and Evaluation Service. http://www.ed.gov/offices/OUS/PES/index.html

U.S. Department of Justice, Bureau of Justice Assistance (BJA), Evaluation Website. http://www.ojp.usdoj.gov/BJA/evaluation/

U.S. Department of Justice (DOJ), Office of Juvenile Justice and Delinquency Prevention (OJJDP), Juvenile Justice Evaluation Center. http://www.jrsa.org/jjec/index.html

U.S. Department of Health and Human Services, Administration for Children and Families, Office of Planning, Research and Evaluation (OPRE). http://www.acf.dhhs.gov/programs/opre/

U.S. Department of Health and Human Services (DHHS), Office of the Assistant Secretary for Planning and Evaluation. http://aspe.os.dhhs.gov/

U.S. Department of Health and Human Services (DHHS), Office of the Inspector General (OIG), Office of Evaluation and Inspections (OEI). http://www.os.dhhs.gov/progorg/oei/

U.S. Environmental Protection Agency, Evaluation of Environmental Programs. http://www.epa.gov/evaluate/

U.S. Environmental Protection Agency, Office of Inspector General, Independent Evaluation of Environmental Programs. http://www.epa .gov/oig/organization/ope.htm

National Organizations Working on Nonprofit Evaluation

Grantmakers for Effective Organizations (GEO) is a membership organization of funders that develops new content, programs, and services for funders interested in improving nonprofit performance. Founded in 1997, GEO merged with Grantmakers Evaluation Network in 2002, enhancing the resources available to help grantmakers achieve measurable results. GEO publishes the *Due Diligence Tool* and *Evaluation as a Pathway to Learning*, both available for free download. GEO also has a good list of resource links on its Website. http://www.geofunders.org/

The Leader to Leader Institute's mission is to strengthen the leadership of the social sector. Established in 1990 as the Peter F. Drucker Foundation for Nonprofit Management, the Institute provides social sector leaders with the essential leadership wisdom, inspiration, and resources to lead for innovation and to build vibrant social sector nonprofit organizations. http://www.pfdf.org/

The Alliance for Nonprofit Management is the result of the 1997 merger of the Nonprofit Management Association and Support Centers of America. Members include management support organizations, individual professionals, and national and regional organizations that provide technical assistance to nonprofits. http://www.allianceonline.org

The Council for Nonprofit Innovation (CNI) was started in 2000 by the conservative Performance Institute, dedicated to enhancing the transparency, accountability, and overall performance of organizations in the nonprofit sector. CNI improves the capacity of foundations and nonprofit organizations to manage, evaluate, and improve their bottom-line impact and performance. http://www.cniweb.org/

Fieldstone Alliance is a publishing and consulting organization that spun out of the work of the Wilder Foundation of Minnesota. Fieldstone publishes many of the best how-to books on nonprofit management, including a few on evaluation. http://www.fieldstonealliance.org

The Urban Institute was founded in 1968 to provide independent
nonpartisan analysis of the problems facing America's cities and their
residents. The institute analyzes policies, evaluates programs, and informs
community development to in all 50 states and in over 28 countries.
The Urban Institute has two centers that provide information relevant
to nonprofit organizations and evaluation. http://www.urban.org

The Center on Nonprofits & Philanthropy (CNP) conducts and disseminates
research on the role and impact of nonprofit organizations and philanthropy. In addition, CNP conducts research on and analyzes trends in the
operations and finances of U.S. charitable organizations through data
developed and maintained by its National Center for Charitable Statistics
(NCCS) and other sources. http://www.urban.org/center/cnp/index.cfm

The Income & Benefits Policy Center studies how public policy influences
the behavior and economic well-being of families, particularly the disabled,
the elderly, and those with low incomes. Scholars look at income support,
social insurance, tax, child-support, and employee-benefit programs.
http://www.urban.org/center/ibp/index.cfm

Books

There a large number of proven evaluation and research instruments
included in books that are available from university libraries. Accessing these
will require some research, but they will provide you with questionnaires,
interview forms, and other items that have been developed in the field and
tested by professional researchers.

If you live near a research university, the social services librarian can
be an invaluable resource for finding volumes of evaluation and research
instruments. Make an appointment in advance. If you're not connected with
the university, explain that you're working with a community organization
undertaking a major project and are looking for information to help with
your evaluation. Ask the librarian for advice on other evaluation resources
as well as tests and questionnaires.

Many of these works appear in book lists that can be accessed online.
For example, the following two university libraries have developed expensive
lists of books containing test questionnaires in various fields. I'm sure there
are other such sites at other universities, maybe even one near you.

University of Texas at Austin

Tests and Measures in the Social Sciences: A Listing of Books Containing Tests and Questionnaires in Various Fields. This clumsy-looking work-in-progress lists over 100 books containing over 10,000 instruments. By clicking the link beside each volume, you can see a list of the instruments it contains. http://libraries.uta.edu/helen/Test&meas/testmainframe.htm

St. Louis University

Resource Guide of Instrumentation, Tests and Measures. In addition to the books list, the site has links to over 100 commercial test development companies and other test related information. http://pages.slu.edu/faculty/josephme/resguides/tests.html#Internet

Glossary

activities: What a program does to fulfill its mission; that is, the services it provides.

analysis: The process of systematically applying statistical techniques and logic to interpret, compare, categorize, and summarize data collected in order to draw conclusions.

anonymity: Ensuring that information cannot be traced back to the person who provided it. (*Compare with* confidentiality.)

association: When two variables are related and change together.

attribution: The process of identifying the single or multiple factors responsible for an observed outcome; for example, program participation reduced stress by 50 percent.

attrition: Loss of subjects from the defined sample during the course of a study.

audiences: Those people who will be guided by the evaluation in making decisions and others who have a stake in the evaluation. (*See* stakeholders.)

average: A number that typifies a group of numbers. Three common types are mean, median, and mode.

baseline: Facts gathered about the condition or performance of subjects prior to treatment or intervention, used to measure changes during and after the program.

benchmarks: Performance data from similar organizations that are used for comparison for setting organizational program goals.

best practice: A management idea that asserts that there exists a technique, method, or process that is more effective at delivering a particular outcome than any other technique, method, or process.

black box evaluation: Used to describe evaluation designs that measure indicators of outcomes without examining the process or articulating a program theory.

case study: A detailed description and analysis of a single project or program in the context of its environment.

causal: When a series of events, thoughts, or actions result in a particular event or individual outcome.

cluster evaluation: Projects are designated as a cluster because they support similar strategies, serve the same target population, or collectively address a specific outcome, such as systemic institutional or policy changes. Cluster evaluations examine such a cluster of projects to determine how well they achieve the broad goals of a programming initiative.

code: To translate a given set of data or items into a set of quantitative or qualitative symbols.

cohort analysis: The analysis of data about a particular group, such as comparing successive groups passing through a program. For example, using subjects scheduled to receive services (a wait list) as a control or comparison group for those actively receiving services.

comparison group: A comparison group is not subjected to treatment (independent variable), thus creating a means for comparison with the experimental group that does receive the treatment.

confidentiality: Keeping information that could link participants to their responses private, available only to designated personnel for specific evaluation needs. (*Compare with* anonymity.)

context (of an evaluation): The combination of the factors accompanying the study that may have influenced its results.

control group: A randomly selected group as similar as possible to an experimental group (one that is exposed to a program), and exposed to all the conditions of the investigation except the program being studied.

correlation: How two related variables change together; i.e., direction (positive or negative) and whether the change is statistically significant.

cost-benefit analysis: A type of analysis that compares the costs and benefits of programs, translated into monetary terms.

cost-effectiveness analysis: A type of analysis that compares the effectiveness of different interventions by comparing their costs and outcomes measured in physical units (e.g., number of children immunized or the number of deaths averted) rather than in monetary units.

cross-site evaluation: A joint evaluation of several programs, often funded through the same source, to compare and assess the effectiveness of different program models. Sometimes participation is required as part of receiving a federal grant.

data: Material gathered during the course of a program evaluation, which serves as the basis for information, discussion, and inference.

data analysis: The process of systematically applying statistical and logical techniques to describe, summarize, and compare data.

database: An accumulation of information that has been systematically organized for easy access and analysis; usually computerized.

demographic information: Descriptive data that includes race and/or ethnicity, gender, age, grade level, socioeconomic status, and similar kinds of information.

dissemination: The process of communicating either the procedures or the lessons learned from an evaluation in a timely, unbiased, and consistent manner.

document review: The examination of records or documents that contain information about the context in which a program occurs, about people's behavior, and about other relevant conditions or events.

effectiveness: A measure of the extent to which a program achieves its planned results (outputs, outcomes, and goals).

efficiency: A measure of how economically or optimally inputs (financial, human, technical, and material resources) are used to produce outputs.

empowerment evaluation: Uses an outside evaluator to assist the program staff in conducting a self-evaluation and using the results to improve their program.

evaluability: The extent to which an activity or a program can be evaluated in a reliable and credible fashion, with available resources and within the proposed timeframe.

evaluation: The systematic collection of information about the activities, characteristics, and outcomes of a program to make judgments about the program, improve program effectiveness, and/or inform decisions about future programming.

evidence: The information used to support conclusions.

evidence-based practice (EBP): Interventions that show consistent scientific evidence of promoting improved client outcomes.

experiment: Tests the existence of causal relationships by comparing outcomes for subjects randomly assigned to program services with outcomes of subjects randomly assigned to alternative services or no services.

experimental design: The plan of an evaluation, including selection of subjects, order of administration of the experimental treatment, the kind of treatment, the procedures by which it is administered, and the recording of the data (with special reference to the particular statistical analyses to be performed).

external evaluation: Activities undertaken by a person or group outside the organization to determine the success of a program.

external events: What happens when events outside the project influence participant outcomes. Also called *effect of history*.

external validity: The generalizability of study results to other groups, settings, treatments, and outcomes.

face validity: The assumption that an instrument measures what it is intended to measure, because it seems to make sense. The best judges of face validity are people with knowledge of the subject matter. When a new instrument (such as a survey) is designed, it may be circulated to experts to determine its face validity before being field-tested.

fidelity scale: An instrument used to verify that an intervention is being implemented in a manner consistent with the original treatment model.

field test: The study of a program, project, or instructional material in settings like those where it is to be used.

finding: A factual statement on a program based on empirical evidence gathered through monitoring and evaluation activities.

five-point scale: A questionnaire design that uses opposing adjectives on ends of a scale, with ranking between; for example: Easy 1 2 3 4 5 Difficult.

focus group: A group selected for its relevance to an evaluation that is engaged by a trained facilitator in a series of discussions designed for sharing insights, ideas, and observations on a topic of concern. A set of questions is often used that is focused to move the discussion toward concepts of interest to the investigator.

formal interview: A conversation in which the evaluator obtains information from a respondent or group of respondents by asking a set of specific questions.

formative evaluation: A type of process evaluation undertaken during program implementation to furnish information that will guide program improvement. Similar to process evaluation.

front-end evaluation: *See* needs assessment.

generalizability: The extent to which information about a program, project, or instructional material collected in one setting can be used to reach a valid judgment about how it will perform in other settings.

goal: The general purpose of a project, stated in broad terms.

goal attainment scaling tool: A tool used in counseling where specific goals for a client are set jointly between a case worker and client as part of a case management process.

grounded theory: A method similar to qualitative evaluation, in which the researcher doesn't start with a theory; rather, the theory is developed inductively, based on observations that are summarized into conceptual categories, evaluated and generally refined, and linked to other conceptual categories.

impact evaluation: Evaluation focused on the effect of a program with the intention of being able to attribute any observed changes to the program.

indicator: A specific, observable, and measurable characteristic or change that shows the progress a program is making toward achieving a desired outcome.

informed consent: Agreement by the participants in an evaluation of the use of their names and/or confidential information supplied by them in specified ways, for stated purposes, and in light of possible consequences prior to the collection and/or release of this information in evaluation reports.

inputs: The resources a program uses to implement a program. Examples are staff, volunteers, facilities, equipment, curricula, and money.

institutional review board (IRB): A group of organizational and community representatives required by federal law to review the ethical issues in all federally funded research that involves human subjects. Some types of evaluation may be considered research under this requirement.

instrument: An assessment device adopted, adapted, or constructed for the purpose of the evaluation.

internal evaluation: An examination of program activities conducted in-house by staff.

internal validity: The accuracy of the data in reflecting the reality of a program.

interrupted time series: Compares trends in outcomes before and after the program.

intervention: The program or treatment that is being evaluated.

interview: A conversation in which the evaluator obtains information from a respondent or group of respondents.

key informants: Individuals who have special knowledge about identified issues.

lessons learned: Learning from experience that is applicable to a generic situation rather than to a specific circumstance.

Likert scale: A psychometric scale often used on questionnaires, which asks respondents to specify their agreement with each of a series of attachments; for example: 1. Strongly agree, 2. Agree, 3. Neutral, 4. Disagree, 5. Strongly disagree.

logic model: A flowchart that summarizes the key elements of a program: resources, activities, outputs, outcomes, and goals. A logic model also shows assumed cause-and-effect linkages among elements of the model, according to a theory of change.

longitudinal data: Observations collected over a period of time.

longitudinal evaluation: An evaluation that measures changes by collecting a series of data over time, sometimes including follow-up months or years after the program is completed.

manualized program: A program that has adopted an evidence-based practice, in which its intervention is codified in a written protocol or manual.

mean: The arithmetic average of a group of numbers, derived by adding all the values and dividing by the number of values.

median: The midpoint in a group of numbers, from which half are larger and half are smaller.

meta-evaluation: A study of a series of evaluations or research studies to look for commonalities, differences, and trends.

milestones: Predesignated interim goals used to measure program progress.

mixed method design: Evaluation design involving the planned use of both quantitative and qualitative methods.

mode: An average that represents the most frequently found number in a group.

multivariate analysis: A process that statistically matches subjects on variables such as age, education, and income and determines whether there is still a significant difference between the project and comparison groups (e.g., percentage of students graduating from high school).

multivariate regression: *See* regression analysis.

needs assessment: Information collected before a program is planned or implemented to identify needs and target audiences and to develop appropriate strategies. Sometimes referred to as *front-end* or *preliminary evaluation.*

negative case analysis: Identifying those clients for whom a program didn't work for and doing extensive interviews to try to determine the causes of failure.

normative evaluation: An evaluation comparing a program to a pre-established norm such as benchmarks or an evidence-based practice.

objectives: Statements describing the results to be achieved and the manner in which these results will be achieved.

observation: In-person, firsthand examination of program participants and activities.

outcome evaluation, outcome-based evaluation: Focuses on the changes occurring in participants after the program.

outcomes: Changes in clients or communities resulting from program activities and outputs.

outputs: Products of a program's activities, such as the number of meals provided, classes taught, or participants served. Also called *units of service.*

outside evaluation: *See* external evaluation.

paradigm: A perspective or point of view affecting what is recognized, known, or valued and done.

participatory evaluation: Involves staff and other stakeholders in the design and implementation of the evaluation process in order to have their perspectives considered, with the evaluation being done by an outside evaluator.

performance monitoring: An evaluation strategy that looks at quantitative indicators of program or service delivery. It doesn't necessarily judge quality or outcomes, but whether the organization is delivering the intended outputs.

population: All the people in a particular group.

pre- and post-program design: Measures and compares outcomes before and after a program.

preliminary evaluation: *See* needs assessment.

principal investigator: The person in charge of conducting a program or evaluation.

probe: Follow-up questions asked during an interview to help get at key issues and clarify the respondent's answers.

process evaluation: Evaluation that describes implementation of a program, that is, the activities undertaken as part of a program. Similar to formative evaluation.

program: A time-bound intervention that comprises an entire operation, utilizing resources and producing program activities, outputs, and outcomes.

program theory: A theory or model of how a program is expected to cause the intended or observed outcomes. Developed using logic models.

project: A time-bound intervention that consists of a set of planned, interrelated activities aimed at achieving defined program outputs.

protocol: A set of instructions used as a guide for conducting observations or interviews to help ensure that the appropriate information is collected from each respondent.

qualitative evaluation: Gathers information to capture the experience of participants, but which cannot necessarily be quantified. It asks questions like "How?" and "Why?"

qualitative methods (QUAL): Evaluation methods such as participant observation, intensive interviewing, and focus groups that are designed to capture social life as participants experience it, rather than in categories predetermined by the evaluator. Results are often expressed in narrative as opposed to numbers.

quantitative evaluation: Gathers data that can be put in numeric terms for statistical analysis. It asks the questions "How much?" and "How frequently?"

quantitative methods (QUAN): Evaluation methods such as surveys and experiments that record variation on social life in terms of categories that vary in amount and can be interpreted as numbers or put into order for statistical analysis.

quasi-experimental design: Evaluation designs that do not involve randomly assigning members of the target population to either an intervention or a comparison group. Typical quasi-experimental designs include pre- and post-program designs, comparison group designs, and interrupted time series designs.

questionnaire: The written instrument used to collect information as part of a survey.

random sampling: Selecting a number of people from a larger group or population so that every individual has an equal probability to be chosen.

rates under treatment: The estimate of future service needs based on current client data, including service usages and a waiting list.

regression analysis: Models the relationship between one or more dependent variables (usually termed Y) and the independent variables (usually termed $X_1, \ldots, Xp$). With more than one dependent variable, we speak of *multivariate regression*.

regression effect: The tendency of examinee who scored above or below the mean of a distribution on a pretest to score closer to the mean on the posttest.

reliability: Consistency and dependability of data collected through repeated use of a scientific instrument or data collection procedure under the same conditions.

response rate: The number of people who respond to a questionnaire compared with the number of people who received the questionnaire.

rigor: Refers to the strength of the data in demonstrating causality.

sample: A subset that is similar in characteristics to the larger group from which it is selected.

sampling error: Any difference between the characteristics of a sample and characteristics of a population. The larger the sampling error, the less representative the sample.

secondary data: Data that was not collected by the evaluator.

secondary data analysis: A reanalysis of data to verify the accuracy of the results of the initial analysis or to answer different questions.

self-report instrument: A device in which people make and report judgments about the functioning of their project, program, or instructional material.

significant difference: A likelihood that an observed difference between two statistics probably did not occur by chance.

snowball samples: Technique used to increase the sample size of a difficult-to-reach group by asking members to identify other members of the group.

social indicators: The existing statistics and markers used to study the condition of a target population, such as school dropout rate or child abuse reports.

stakeholders: People, groups, or entities that have a role and interest in the aims and implementation of a program.

standardization: Typically involves developing a manual book that clearly defines the practice so that it can be replicated, and measures to assess whether the intervention is being practiced accurately. (*See* fidelity scale.)

statistic: A summary number that is typically used to described a characteristic of a sample.

summative evaluation: A type of evaluation in which results are used at the end of a project to judge its success and impact by comparison with its goals and objectives.

survey: Systematic collection of information from a defined population, usually by means of interviews or questionnaires.

sustainability: Durability of program results after the end of a grant period.

theory-based evaluation: Starts with the premise that every program has an underlying theory, often described in a logic model. The evaluation is designed to see whether the program produces the goals and outcomes from the logic model.

theory of change: A systematic assessment of what happens in a program to make desired outcomes occur, often shown in a logic model.

time series study: A study in which periodic measurements are obtained prior to, during, and following the introduction of an intervention in order to assess the effect of the intervention.

tracer studies: Contacting neighbors, relatives, friends, and other associates to locate people who have moved.

transparency: Carefully describing and sharing information, rationales, assumptions, and procedures as the basis for value judgments and decisions.

triangulation: The use of multiple sources and methods to gather similar information in order to improve the validity of evaluation findings.

units of service: *See* outputs.

utility: The extent to which an evaluation produces and disseminates reports that inform relevant audiences and have beneficial impact on their work.

validity: The extent to which methodologies and instruments measure what they are supposed to measure. (*See* external validity, face validity, internal validity.)

variable: A characteristic that can take on different values.

The author gratefully acknowledges these sources of information for the Glossary definitions:

Benchmarking for Nonprofits: How to Measure, Manage and Improve Performance by Jason Saul. Fieldstone Alliance (2004).

Handbook of Practical Program Evaluation (2nd edition), editors Joseph S. Wholey, Harry P. Hatry, and Kathryn E. Newcomer. John Wiley & Sons (2004).

Investigating the Social World: The Process and Practice of Research (4th edition) by Russell K. Schutt. Pine Forge Press/Sage (2004).

The Manager's Guide to Program Evaluation: Planning, Contracting and Managing for Useful Results by Paul W. Mattessich, PhD. Fieldstone Alliance (2003).

Measuring Program Outcomes: A Practical Approach. United Way of America (1996).

Programme Manager's Planning, Monitoring & Evaluation Toolkit. United Nations Population Fund (2004).

RealWorld Evaluation: Working Under, Budget, Time, Data, and Political Constraints by Michael Bamberger, Jim Rugh, and Linda Mabry. Sage (2006).

Taking Stock: A Practical Guide to Evaluating Your Own Programs by Sally Boyd and Kathleen Rapp. Horizon Research (1997).

When & How to Use External Evaluators by Tracey Rutnik and Marty Campbell. Baltimore Area Grantmakers (2002).

Annotated Bibliography

Benchmarking for Nonprofits: How to Measure, Manage and Improve Performance by Jason Saul. Fieldstone Alliance (2004).

The Chicago Guide to Writing about Numbers: The Effective Presentation of Quantitative Information by Jane E. Miller. University of Chicago Press (2004).

The Grantseekers Guide to Project Evaluation (2nd edition), Jacqueline Ferguson, editor. Aspen Publishers (1999)—An education-oriented approach with a good set of guidelines for evaluation planning and a strong emphasis on statistics.

Grant Winner's Toolkit: Project Management and Evaluation by James A. Quick and Cheryl C. New. John Wiley & Sons, New York (2000)—A good how-to overview, with lots of charts and forms for data collection.

Handbook of Practical Program Evaluation (2nd edition), Joseph S. Wholey, Harry P. Hatry, and Kathryn E. Newcomer, editors. John Wiley & Sons (2004).

How to Use Qualitative Methods in Evaluation by Michael Quinn Patton. Sage Publications (1987).

Investigating the Social World: The Process and Practice of Research (4th edition) by Russell K. Schutt. Pine Forge Press/Sage (2004)—Before evaluation there was research, and if you really want to learn evaluation, you have to understand social science research. This excellent college textbook is a good place to start.

The Manager's Guide to Program Evaluation: Planning, Contracting and Managing for Useful Results by Paul W. Mattessich, PhD. Fieldstone Alliance (2003).

Outcomes for Success! by Judith Clegg, MSW, and Jane Reissman, PhD. The Evaluation Forum, Organizational Research Services, Inc., Seattle, Washington (1995, 2000), http://www.organizationalresearch.com— This book explains how to develop your own outcome-based program evaluation, including use of a logic model. I like the 1995 edition for its logic model formats, but the 2005 edition has more in-depth discussion of evaluation.

Practical Grant Writing and Program Evaluation by Francis Yuen and Kenneth Terao. Brooks/Cole-Thomson (2003)—An excellent resource, but follows the authors' own model and terminology.

The Process of Program Evaluation by John Van Maanen. The Grantsmanship Center (1979)—John runs on a bit, but if you can get past the academic style, this is a good short overview.

RealWorld Evaluation: Working Under, Budget, Time, Data, and Political Constraints by Michael Bamberger, Jim Rugh, and Linda Mabry. Sage (2006)—An excellent overview of program evaluation, plus it delivers on the problems identified in the title.

Free Downloads

A Guide to Evaluation Primers produced by the Association for the Study and Development of Community (ASDC) for the Robert Wood Johnson Foundation—This document offers an orientation to handbooks and basic primers on evaluation. These resources are designed to meet the needs of the non-expert.

Logic Model Development Guide. W.K. Kellogg Foundation (2001)—This guide is available from http://www.wkkf.org.

Planning and Using Survey Research Projects by Diane Colasanto, PhD, of Princeton Survey Research Associates (PSRA)—Survey research can be a powerful tool. If you want advice on designing your survey or hiring a survey expert, start here. Intended for a general audience and available free for download from http://www.rwjf.org/research/toolsresources.jhtml.

Program Evaluation: Principles and Practices by Sherril Gelmon, Anna Foucek, and Amy Waterbury. Northwest Health Foundation (2005)—An excellent how-to book for designing and doing basic evaluation. Available free for download from www.nwhf.org.

W.K. Kellogg Evaluation Handbook. This 117-page volume from one of America's largest and most evaluation-oriented foundations discusses both the theory and practice of evaluation. Available free for download as an Adobe Acrobat file or for ordering as a paper copy from http://www.wkkf.org/.

Index

A
academic evaluators, 90
activities, program
  definition, 123
  in logic model, 66
  in program logic model, 68–70
AIR (American Institutes for Research), 111
Alliance for Nonprofit Management, 120
American Evaluation Association, 118
American Factfinder, 111
American Institutes for Research (AIR), 111
analysis, 123
anonymity, 25, 123
application guidelines, 46–47, 59
association, 33, 123
Association of Baltimore Area Grantmakers, 93
attribution, 123
attrition, 123
audience, 75–76, 123
average, 123

B
baseline, 86–87, 123
behavioral interview, 18
benchmark, 86, 123
benchmark statements, 72
best practices
  definition, 85, 123
  resources, 112–113
  what funders want, 43, 46
BJA (Bureau of Justice Assistance), 119
black box evaluation, 123
blueprint program. *See* evidence-based practice
  (EBP)
board of directors as evaluators, 9–10
Boess, Maryn, 62
bookstores, as resources, 115
Bureau of Justice Assistance (BJA), 119
Byrne (Edward) Memorial Grant Program, 87

C
C%D (cumulative percentage distribution), 30
capability statement, 61
capital funding, 8
case study, 123
causal, 123
causal inference, 25
CDC (Centers for Disease Control and
  Prevention), 119
CDC's Best Practices of Youth Violence
  Prevention, 113

CDC Wonder, 112
census, resources, 111
CensusScope, 111
Center for Learning Excellence, 113
Center for Mental Health Services (CMHS), 119
Center for Substance Abuse Treatment (CSAT),
  54–57
Center for What Works, 113
Center on Nonprofits and Philanthropy (CNP),
  121
central tendency, measures of, 31–32
CFD (cumulative frequency distribution), 30
change statements, 72
CharityChannel, 62
checklist, 16
Children's Investment Fund, 85
Childtrends, 113
City-Data, 111
cluster evaluation, 124
CMHS (Center for Mental Health Services), 119
CNI (Council for Nonprofit Innovation), 120
CNP (Center on Nonprofits and Philanthropy),
  121
Coalition for Evidence-Based Policy, 113
code, 124
cohort analysis, 124
commitment to evaluation, 4, 10, 70
common grant application, 49–50
communication, 28, 93
Community Toolbox, 118
comparison group, 124
conceptual interview, 18
confidentiality, 25, 124
constant-comparative analysis, 36
content analysis, 35–36
context, 124
continuous quality improvement (CQI), 10
control group, 124
correlation, 33, 124
cost-benefit analysis, 19–21, 124
cost effectiveness, 42
cost-effectiveness analysis, 19–21, 124
cost of evaluation
  evaluability and, 23
  objective to evaluation, 6
  whether to include in budget, 47
Council for Nonprofit Innovation (CNI), 120
County & City Databook, 111
Cowles Foundation example, 48
CQI (continuous quality improvement), 10
credibility and outside evaluation, 89
cross-site evaluation, 124

About the Author

Michael Wells has been working with nonprofits for over 30 years as staff, volunteer, board member, and consultant. In the early 1980s, he realized that he "had been working with all of these people in nonprofits who wanted to do good in the world and not spend all of their time thinking about money. But they spent all of their time thinking about money."
He got a job as a development director to learn how to raise funds, and after a couple of development staff positions, began consulting on grants in 1987.

Michael has worked with dozens of nonprofit agencies, health clinics, Native American tribes, school districts, and local governments, and has helped them raise over $50 million. His background in all aspects of nonprofit management gives him a broad perspective of organizational needs. His stints in the business world as a journalist and salesman help him recognize differences and similarities in the sectors. He likes grantwriting because it combines the opportunity to do good in the world with the chance to learn about a wide variety of subjects: "I get to develop all of these wonderful projects and get them funded, but I don't have to run them."

Michael is a partner in the consulting firm Grants Northwest. He is a Certified Fund Raising Executive (CFRE) and has a master's degree in humanities. He is a faculty member at Portland State University, where he teaches grantwriting. He is editor of the online CharityChannel *Grants and Foundation Review* and a national board member of the Grant Professionals Certification Institute (GPCI). He lives with his wonderful wife Julie in Portland, Oregon. He has three grown daughters and three grandchildren.

Grants publications available from Portland State University
Continuing Education Press.

GRANTWRITING BEYOND THE BASICS Series by Michael K. Wells
Book 1. Proven Strategies Professionals Use to Make Their Proposals Work
Book 2. Understanding Nonprofit Finances
Book 3. Successful Program Evaluation
(Books 4 and 5 coming soon.)

GETTING FUNDED: The Complete Guide to Writing Grant Proposals
by Dr. Mary Hall & Susan Howlett

For more information on these and our other publications, and to order,
please go to www.cep.pdx.edu, or call us toll-free at 1-866-647-7377.

Coming in Fall 2008

The next book in the Grantwriting Beyond the Basics series, *The Other Side of the Fence*, will look at the grants world from the point of view of funders, both public and private.

Who will be profiled:

- Foundation staff
- Foundation trustees
- Federal program officers
- Federal grant reviewers
- Local government contract managers
- Community foundation boards.

What will be described:

- What happens inside foundation board meetings
- What happens to your proposal as it works through the federal decision process
- A typical day in the life of foundation program staff
- A typical day in the life of federal program staff
- What it's like to be a government grant reviewer
- Funders likes and complaints in grant proposals
- What program officers look for in site visits.

How to use the information:

- Building and maintaining relationships
- How this relates to record keeping, maintaining appropriate roles
- How consultants' relationships are different from in-house grantwriters
- How relationships are different with foundation staff, foundation trustees, and government staff
- Networking and getting and using referrals and introductions.